A GROWING GENIUS

CHRIS McKIMM

Paperback: 978-1-964035-71-0
eBook: 978-1-964035-72-7
Library of Congress Control Number: 2025904584

This is a work of nonfiction.

SWEETSPIRE LITERATURE
——— MANAGEMENT ———

TABLE OF CONTENTS

CHAPTER ONE

Time takes the pain away
That's what my friends all say
But I still think of you each day
It's the same for everyone
black clouds across the sun
but my life is less by more than one

My earliest memory of my brother is watching him being breastfed by our mother. I feel memories rather than see them. She seemed so beautiful, and he seemed so content.

My brother and I were RAAF brats—perpetual outsiders. I went to ten schools; he was lucky and only went to six. Our peripatetic childhood saw us living in many houses on many streets, in areas as disparate as 1960s Oklahoma and Bullsbrook, Western Australia.

It was a matter of wondering, "Where are we this week, Daddy?"

There was no continuity in our childhoods. One learns the habits of non-commitment and escape. We were always moving somewhere "far away," and whatever was achieved here would be regarded with suspicion and contempt there. So why do anything here?

It was a constant case of learning new conventions and reshaping oneself to fit the new paradigm. Often, this process was thoroughly discombobulating and destructive to whatever it is that makes up the "self."

To this day, my behavior is considered arrogant. If I walk into a crowded room, I feel I'm walking into a hostile playground, where I am the last thing desired. Eventually, one accepts that the mores of each place are as arbitrary and illogical—often in contrast to one another—as anywhere else. Yet wherever we were, it was presumed to be the best of places. But to my brother and me, each place felt just as inconsequential and insular as the last town the Air Force took the fighter pilot and his family.

We grew up with an "us against them" attitude. It bred a subconscious insularity that meant we found solace and reason within the confines of our small family—and more particularly, for my brother and me, in each other.

I vividly remember lunchtimes at new schools: after a morning with hostile, patronizing strangers, I would wait to see his big-headed, round face greeting me with a transcendent smile.

I realized at an early age that my brother was an exceptional human being. More intelligent than I, he could rise above the petty vagaries of life and love being alive. He thought I was cleverer than I was and would try to help me see that I was better than I believed—and that I could achieve his noble detachment.

> *I still see you on the cold, tiled floor*
> *frozen, I stand at the door*
> *I cannot believe what I am seeing*
> *But I have seen it all before.*

The phone call came abruptly at three in the morning. "Something's happened to Tony."

I lived just three doors away. I rushed to his house and found him slumped in the corner of the small bathroom—utterly out of place, like a sculpture abandoned mid-fall.

As soon as I saw him, I knew he was gone. No one alive could fold into themselves like that.

I tried to move him. I wanted to give him mouth-to-mouth, to bring him back. But he was so heavy. I remember thinking, *Is this what they mean by a "dead weight"?*

After a painful struggle, I managed to get him horizontal on the tiled floor. I pushed air into his lungs. What came back was a soft, awful sound—something between a sigh and a rattle. The breath of absence. I burst into tears.

Demonic sounds erupted from my throat—raw, primal, and unrecognizable. My heart lay crushed on those cold tiles, shattered and, as I would come to learn, irretrievably broken.

His massive head, crowned with long, luxurious hair, lay in the crook of my arm. I screamed at him. *How could you leave me? How could you do this to me?*

I was unhinged. Hysterical. Envious, even, that he had found a way out—and I had not.

A part of me wanted to go with him. A part of me knew something inside me had died, too.

We had lived for music. He was a genius guitarist. I remember him endlessly working on "Clementine" before morphing into the flashiest lead player in any room. From his bedroom, melodies would drift out like spells, and I'd wonder if some of that magic might live in me too.

It did. Soon I was awkwardly strumming chords, inventing my own rhythms.

A friend at university showed me a few basic chords. I didn't see him again until the year's end, when we crossed paths at a party. I was in a corner, playing guitar. He came up to me and said: "Hey Chris, I can see you're not a beginner anymore—you're just shit house." Some things stick with you. It was a backhanded compliment, but I got the message. I had a long way to go.

When my brother and I played together, he was incredibly encouraging. I didn't listen closely enough. I could have learned so much more—been so much better. But I didn't.

I started writing songs as soon as I could form a chord. Conservatively, I've written over a thousand. The best of them could stand beside anyone's. But fear and circumstance have kept them unheard.

> *Paul and I have been writing songs*
> *For most of our lives*
> *Millions know his tunes*
> *Nearly nobody knows mine*
> *But both of us are driven by*
> *The very same desire*
> *The mystery of melody*
> *Hiding new surprise*

But my brother was hugely encouraging of my songwriting. A mutual friend once told me that Tony had said his greatest pleasure in music was *"working on my brother's songs."* I'd always assumed he was just doing me a favor—like he did for so many others.

Musically, he was always there to help. Countless people had their lives changed by his generous introduction to music. But if I had known that *I* was the heart of his musical joy, I might have let down my guard. I might have been less defensive.

I ache when I think of all the times I rejected his help. I remember, vividly, the day he tried to show me a lick on the guitar. It was something he found effortless, but I struggled. Eventually, I gave up—frustrated, embarrassed—and muttered that I just couldn't do it.

He'd tried so patiently. But after one too many refusals, he laid his guitar down, looked me squarely in the eye, and said, with quiet resignation: *"Honestly, sometimes I don't know why I bother."*

In that moment, he saw me the way I feared the world saw me: as a negative, underachieving version of myself. And I saw the pain my defensiveness had caused him.

> *This is an early song*
> *I used to play with him*
> *and though he tried so hard*
> *I would not let him in*
> *What I'm trying to say*
> *Is I usually wrong*
> *And I'm so very sorry*
> *Anthony John*

Some years after his death, I made the mistake of reading a letter he had written to our parents. In it, he spoke at length about our musical (non)relationship and revealed, with heartbreaking clarity, the depth of his commitment to me—his need for us to be together.

Until then, I had forgotten that I was his big brother. That I was, in some ways, a role model.

Reading that letter, I realized what I had missed. I had always assumed he knew I believed *he* was the clever one—and that anything I did, by comparison, was clumsy and pedestrian.

Where I would crawl, he would fly.

But even so, he was endlessly encouraging. And when I was with him, I felt good. I felt big. I felt strong.

> *Did I say to you*
> *It was such a privilege to*
> *Stand with you and sing our songs*
> *I know what I would do*
> *If I had the power to*
> *I'd bring it back inside this song.*

There are days when I think he is standing on my shoulder. He is watching over me, and I see him as my guardian angel these days.

> *So, if you see me fall apart*
> *Hover over me*
> *Mend my broken heart*
> *Guide my way*
> *and light the dark*
> *I need a guardian angel*
> *be my guardian angel.*

When John Lennon was shot, someone said they couldn't imagine a world that hadn't known him. I understand that.

But what breaks my heart is that my brother—just as talented, just as singular—*was* never known by the world.

Had things gone differently, young guitarists might have studied *him*, as he once studied Page and Clapton. Writers would have celebrated his riffs, his tone, his songs.

But he never wanted fame. When our mother once asked why he didn't pursue a pop career, he replied, "*Mum, would you have me on the charts, squeezed between Rod Stewart and Paper Lace?*"

He saw what was happening to the music world—and turned his back on it. And maybe he was right to.

But maybe, if I hadn't turned my back on *him*, he would have added something unforgettable to the legacy of his generation. The world would have been richer. My life certainly would have.

The world feels smaller without him. I used to feel guilty for thinking about him every day—but I can't help it. Every memory is a collision of joy and regret. Joy for the time we had. Regret for the time we lost. I love you, brother. And I will until the day I die. And when I die, you die again—because my children, and theirs, may never truly know the genius that lives in their blood.

CHAPTER TWO

As his elder brother, I was expected to look down on Tony—literally and figuratively.

In his early years, he was unwell. He was born with a heart defect, so much of my childhood was spent in the care of aunties and a grandmother while he was taken to see "the specialist." He was also born with severely malformed feet and ankles. I remember being told they had to break his ankles to reposition his legs correctly. For the first four years of his life, he wore leg irons; without them, he wouldn't have walked at all.

Like his hands, his feet were large. You could hear the slap of his gait before he entered a room.

I was the athlete; he wasn't. He envied me my physicality just as I envied him his artistry. Not that my athletic career was smooth—myopia was its own handicap. Without my glasses, the world was a blurred and intimidating place. I could only make out detail if it was inches from my face.

In my final year of school, yearning to be accepted by the cool crowd, I decided to try the mindless brutality of Rugby League. My parents disapproved of the sport and refused to buy me boots, so I borrowed an oversized pair from a larger neighbor. At our first second-grade training session, it was revealed I was fantastically fast over thirty meters. I was promptly picked as outside center for the second-grade team and eventually played a few matches for the school's first-grade side.

But my shortsightedness meant I couldn't see the ball clearly until it left the hands of the five-eighth. I was always a few seconds behind the rest—my speed mostly spent just catching up.

I was amazed by the brutality of Rugby League—even at schoolboy level. I'd played AFL in Western Australia earlier in life and remembered it as more nuanced and skillful. Rugby wasn't so much a game as a survival exercise for the relatively uninitiated. Mild-mannered classmates transformed into nostril-flaring bulls. Young men much bigger than me charged headlong, elbows and knees flying, seeking not just to break my tackle but to flatten me entirely.

My tackling technique—if you could call it that—was untutored and mostly involved me leading with my head. It hurt. A lot. I quickly decided I'd finish the season and *never* play again. I made a conscious choice to avoid tackling altogether. Soon enough, defensive plays were called around my absence.

But I kept my spot on the team because I could score tries. I was the top try-scorer in second grade that year, and I scored a few in first grade as well.

My brother saw it all—saw the girls talking to me ("Are you playing this week, Chris?"), and the boys who once ignored me now surrounding me on game day. He must have been jealous. He asked me to help him learn to play.

I didn't think it was a good idea. I tried to explain the cauldron of chaos that was school rugby, and I felt he lacked the size to survive it. But we practiced anyway—in the narrow strip of grass between our house and the neighbor's. There wasn't room for anything fancy, so he just charged at me, over and over. I was two years older and stronger. I tackled hard—too hard. He wasn't fragile, but neither was he robust. And yet, each time I floored him, he got back up. Again and again.

He must've thought I was doing him a favor. That I was toughening him up. And in my ruthless big-brother way, maybe I was. He trusted my intent.

He even tried to innovate. He developed a jumping technique to avoid tackles—essentially trying to leap *over* the tackler. It never worked. Not once. Each time, he went from upright to horizontal or inverted mid-air, crashing to the ground like he'd fallen from orbit. It was painful to watch.

I begged him to stop jumping. He refused. He believed he'd perfect it and change Rugby League history.

I remember watching from the sidelines, his frail frame housing a weak heart, and screaming internally—*don't jump!* And still, he would jump. And each time, as our father would say, his length was measured in the dust or mud of another poorly maintained regional field.

I felt his pain then. I knew I loved him like no one else.

One day, we had argued and parted angrily. He was, in that moment, the classic annoying little brother. I didn't like feeling mad at him—but sometimes, I doubted how deeply I really cared.

Then the phone rang.

A voice I didn't recognize asked, "Are you Chris McKimm?" Something in the tone made my stomach turn. I said yes.

Then came the question: "Is Anthony McKimm your brother?"

I knew instantly that something was very wrong.

The voice on the phone told me he'd come off the front of his motorbike—*my* motorbike, in fact—and that he was lying in the gutter. The caller gave me the street name.

Panicked, I ran to my car. A torrent of questions flooded my mind. Had he been wearing his helmet? He sometimes refused to. I'd told him he *must*, but he'd still go without. And now this.

By the time I reached the scene, police and an ambulance were already there. Tony was sitting upright in the gutter, dazed. His left hand hung at a grotesque angle from the wrist. He'd been playing guitar for years by then—had built a reputation—and when our eyes met, all the anger that had lingered between us vanished. In its place was something else: a love so real it seemed to shimmer around us.

He looked frightened. In pain. And I knew in that instant what was tormenting him. Not the fall, not even the break—it was what this might mean for his guitar playing.

I could see into his soul. His eyes were stripped of bravado or brotherly banter. Just fear and vulnerability. But also relief—*I was there.*

I felt a surge of love for him, deeper than I'd known before. Not just because he was my brother—but because of who he *was*. Funny, inventive, endlessly creative—"leaking music from every pore."

For the rest of his short life, whenever the weather turned cold and he had to play, he would rotate his hand and press the inside of his wrist. The flexibility never fully returned. He insisted it didn't affect his playing, but I could tell he thought it did—and that meant it probably did.

I admired his ambition. I understood his longing to belong to the inner circle. He'd seen me gain acceptance through sport. He wanted his path in, too—with his future resting in his hands. Or rather, in his fingertips.

He wanted to be a drummer.

He begged our parents incessantly for a drum kit. Maybe there was a genetic pull—our father had played drums with Don Burrows as a teenager. His "kit" was a school case with a jumper stretched over it, but still, we could say Dad was Don Burrows' first drummer.

But Dad would hear none of it. No matter how often Tony pleaded, the answer was always no. Maybe it was the thought of all that noise echoing through the suburbs. Whatever it was, the drum kit was off the table.

Eventually, Tony gave up and asked, "What about a guitar?"

Maybe our parents hadn't thought through the implications of an *amplified* electric guitar, but the idea of an acoustic one seemed to strike a chord—excuse the pun. And not long after, a guitar appeared. From then on, there was always a guitar between us.

He took to it like it had been waiting just for him. He and the instrument were inseparable. And it was clear very quickly: he was going to be cool in a way I never had been.

A mutual friend once told me, "Never leave your girlfriend alone with Tony. She won't be your girlfriend in the morning."

Now *he* was the leader of the pack. People sought *him* out to join bands. He and his mates would jam endlessly in a house in Canberra suburbia. Looking back, I wonder if they ever thought, "How do the neighbors put up with this?" But over time, in smoky, booze-drenched parties, they honed their skills and finally became a band.

I got roped in at one point, and soon the band became a vehicle for our songs—mine and Tony's. I was the singer (not good enough to play guitar), and a writer. Tony was just about everything else.

I always felt like an impostor, like I was only there because Tony was my brother. I was never sure whether the rest of the band really respected me. But the chance to stand beside him on stage? Too good to pass up.

We were the brave new Beatles. The Bee Gees with Balls. Australian Crawl that might fly.

There's something about sibling voices. They meld like nothing else. Think of the Everlys. The Bee Gees. Tony and I saw ourselves in that lineage.

He had the most Lennon-like ear for harmony. He didn't just sing the fifth or the third—he'd find melodic counterpoints, usually beneath the melody, giving everything we did a Beatles-esque flavor.

Within the band, *he* was the elder brother. He was the engine, the center of gravity. But I see now: he was as proud to have his brother in the band as I was to be in it.

Not the most confident person, I always looked for reasons I didn't belong. I'd say I had just enough talent to know I didn't have enough talent.

Tony never said otherwise. He didn't need to. Through his quiet persistence, he made it clear: he believed I was wrong about myself.

And he tried to find *me* for *me*.

I stayed lost. I still am. But I will never forget his loving persistence.

His belief in me.

CHAPTER THREE

My earliest memories of Tony are set in Richmond, New South Wales. We lived in a humble house near the end of the strip on the adjoining RAAF base, where our father worked as a pilot.

He was an intimidating, charismatic man—living a boy's own adventure. A larger-than-life Biggles who seemed to fill every room he entered. Each morning, he would leave home to perform aerial feats high above us—high on life and fully absorbed by it. A man who had found his calling, pushing life to its edge.

But at the end of each day, that same man returned to a small, curtain-drawn world: his family. And he struggled to balance those extremes.

I could identify aircraft by sound. The sky was a constant hum of aerial traffic—every day and many nights of "night flying." I could name them without doubt, not to show off, but the way someone says a familiar name. A Neptune. A Wirraway. "Daddy." At the time, he was flying one of only three military helicopters in Australia. If it was him, I'd run outside in hope.

One day, he hovered over our backyard and waved to me.

How fucking fantastic.

How many children—especially in the late fifties—had a father who brought work home like *that*? A whirling, winged Cheshire Cat grinning from above, steady in the air over our yard. It felt like I could reach out and touch him. To this day, it still gives me a thrill.

He was ambitious—driven to get his "arse into the air" no matter what. He loved his wife and two boys, but at times, we were a weight he might've happily flown without. Still, he was a moral man. He gave us a roof, warmth, and structure.

Though a military man, he had a soul. Before all that, he'd played with Don Burrows. Later, he'd serenade his future wife over the phone with slide guitar, learn harmonica, and sing on Perth radio during the early years of WWII. With a maternal grandmother who was a concert pianist and mezzo-soprano, and a paternal grandmother who played piano in silent films, it was inevitable that someone in our family would inherit that legacy.

That someone was my brother.

Though none of us knew it yet, Tony's soul was already singing. He had something of our father's flair, sharp wit, and charm—but with a gentleness that seemed to rise above the shadows of our genetic inheritance.

At this stage of our shared life, I couldn't resist his charm. Still, it hadn't always been love at first sight. I'm told that one day, I emerged triumphantly from the room where he'd been left sleeping—now screaming in shock—and proudly declared, "I pulled him out of his cot."

It's fair to say I resented his presence at first. No longer the center of my parents' world, I now had to share the limelight with a sickly shoo-in whose fragility only made his presence stronger.

My exclusion efforts were unsuccessful because, in 1957, my brother and I excitedly received the news that we were all going to America. In the land of Mickey Mouse and Donald Duck, where people rolled their "R" 's (I remember being given lessons in how to do it), everybody wore big hats, carried guns and drove ridiculously long low cars, some even without tops on them on huge cloverleaf interconnected freeways at super speeds.

CHAPTER FOUR

The gap from the shore to the ship was only gangplank-wide, but the ascent from the wharf to the deck felt vast. At the point of boarding, the sea was a breathtaking distance below. It was dark, mysterious—full of creatures that loomed large in my H.G. Wells-inspired imagination. Tony and I were glad to be with our parents—people we knew loved us and would keep us safe.

Boarding the ship was like stepping into another world—alien, vast. The smell of salt, diesel, and a hint of boiled cabbage filled my nostrils, suggesting things beyond my imagining. The sheer scale of the *SS Orcades*, which was to be our floating home for however long it took to reach America, was overwhelming. I'd probably been told how long the voyage would be, but at that age, time had no shape—life simply moved from one day to the next.

From the wharf, the ship leaned over us like a great, grey beast. It hissed and banged as it prepared for departure, alive with mechanical breath. Workers and crew scurried like ants across the decks and dock, readying the vessel.

I remember Tony and I standing at the ship's railing, looking down at the already distant dock, searching for the extended family who had come to see us off. We threw streamers to them. After several attempts, we managed to connect—to see the other end of a streamer grasped in familiar hands. Hundreds around us were doing the same, holding tightly to paper-thin bonds of what they were leaving behind.

The engines began to roar, vibrations rising through the soles of our shoes as the ship strained against its moorings. We watched the anchor slowly rise into the bow. The streamers stretched to their limits, and as they snapped, people around us fell into tears or silent reflection. Each was left holding a long, limp strand of paper. The sea below became a floating mosaic of red, green, and yellow—streamers falling over themselves, briefly resting atop the waves before becoming waterlogged and disappearing.

The pier looked beautiful—abandoned and bathed in color—but also pitiful and forlorn.

Tony and I had our own cabin, with our parents nearby. We were assigned a porter, a warm, avuncular man who seemed to genuinely enjoy looking after us.

Not long after we left Sydney, our father fell ill. He was diagnosed with chickenpox and sent into quarantine in the bowels of the ship. No one was allowed to see him. My mother fought for access and was eventually allowed to reach him via an exterior crew step ladder. Though discouraged, she insisted—and for years afterward, she dined out on the story of herself in formal dinner dress, gloves and all, climbing up and down that ladder in high heels and high winds.

It was a brave thing for my mother to do, and it spoke volumes about how deeply she loved my father. He often said she lacked a sense of adventure, but surely—even he must have realized that on this occasion, her courage, stubbornness, and devotion were undeniable. She had pushed back against the formal, disapproving British authorities, determined to reach him.

Ironically, as the wife of a fighter pilot, my mother disliked both adventure and heights. This act required both. Even then, she could only see him through a pane of glass. They couldn't hear each other, but at least she knew where he was and that he was being cared for.

There had been criticism of my father—he shouldn't have boarded if he'd been contagious. His response was simple: had he known, he wouldn't have. But that didn't seem to placate the stiff, regulation-bound staff now running our lives.

He returned to us very late in the voyage. I remember that clearly. My mother remembers him being suspicious of our "avuncular" steward. Maybe he questioned the man's motives—or maybe he simply felt guilty for not being there to protect us. But I sometimes wonder: did he suspect something darker? Was he aware of dangers society even then hesitated to name? If so, it would suggest that the issue of child safety—pedophilia—was already a whispered reality in the late 1950s. Some things, sadly, never change.

We, of course, were innocent of all this. Our days were filled with exotic distractions: deck games, endless space to run, and other passengers' cabins to peek into—sometimes even sneak into—with one of us posted as lookout.

There was the great crossing-of-the-equator ceremony. One of the older children informed us, with knowing authority, that "King Neptune" was really a crew member in costume. That made disappointing sense. We pretended we'd known all along. Seated at the pool's edge and surrounded by deckhands dressed like the captain, Neptune would smear children with "ice cream" before they were ceremonially tossed into the pool.

When it was my turn, the sea was calm, and the pool looked like a gentle, blue oasis. I all but leapt in. But when Tony's turn came, the weather had changed. The skies were brooding and stormy. The pool was a churning, punishing cauldron. He looked unsure, but still did what was expected of him. I remember someone lifting him out—quickly, carefully— like a waterlogged doll. A spontaneous round of applause erupted. He looked shaken, drenched, and quietly proud to have endured it.

I don't think Neptune ever smeared fake ice cream on a braver child.

That act of quiet courage would foreshadow something remarkably similar on our return voyage, but that's a story for later.

Despite all the fun and strangeness, every so often, the moist, salty air reminded us exactly where we were—on a metal vessel steaming across the Pacific, a world unto itself.

From the nursery window overlooking the bow, I could watch the ship meet the sea in its most dramatic form. In heavy weather, the vessel would climb impossibly high, revealing only sky, before plunging like a broad blade into the dark valley beyond, slicing open a momentary wound in the ocean. The bow would meet the next mountainous wall of water, briefly suspended in a perfect arc of white spray, before being consumed again. Each time, I thought the ship might split in two. But it never did. Over and over, it rose and fell—defiant, immense.

In front of us were large mock captain's wheels. I adored the illusion of control, the exhilarating sensation that I was steering this heaving leviathan through chaos. In those moments, I was the Captain, entrusted with guiding us to safety. Of course, Tony was beside me, doing the same—both of us captains in command, both equally necessary and heroic in our imagined world.

At night, the phosphorescence in the water painted the crashing waves with an eerie, electric glow. I would watch, mesmerized.

Then came Honolulu. The harbor was quiet. Tony and I stared from our cabin porthole across the gently folding waters toward the shimmering lights of the city. We said nothing, but I felt something shift. A kind of coldness. Not the cold of climate, but of feeling—detachment, maybe. A distance from something unnamable but real.

We were too young to name it then. I can only describe it now as a glimpse of what we would become—two people growing up together and apart. We would learn to mimic connection, to navigate the rituals of closeness, but always with something held back. Always a little separate. Always somewhat alone.

CHAPTER FIVE

Our first view of North America was grey—low-hanging cloud shrouding Vancouver Harbor like a veil. I remember wondering where the sea ended and the sky began. It was January, deep into the northern hemisphere winter. Around us, people moved with hunched shoulders and heads buried in collars. We were likely met by someone from the American Air Force or perhaps a delegate sent on their behalf to guide us through the city to the train station. From there, we'd travel through the Rocky Mountains and down into the vast central plains of the United States.

For Tony and me, there was comfort in the familiar: our parents, and our accents. Around us, the soundscape was suddenly thick with the rolled "r"s we'd been warned about. Everyone seemed to speak deliberately slowly. My father had already been asked to slow down so he could be understood. There couldn't have been many Australian voices in that winter air— we must have sounded as strange to them as they did to us.

Still, we didn't think they were stupid. Just different. But it quickly became clear that they thought we were. They mistook our accents and faster cadence for foolishness. In return, we assumed their slow speech indicated some lack of intelligence. A quiet, mutual condescension had set in.

Then came the silver train, sleek and shining, more bullet than locomotive. It was thrilling to know we would board it, bound for Enid, Oklahoma, where my father had been posted to Vance Air Force Base. His mission was to teach Americans to fly their own T-33 jet trainers.

Even then, it felt a bit like bringing coals to Newcastle. The Americans had practically invented flight. Australia's own early innovators—like Hargreaves and his kites over Stanwell Park—were part of a long tradition of brilliant ideas that rarely became more than that. We were inventive but lacked the critical mass of capital or population to push those ideas forward. Too often, our best inventions were exported, then sold back to us at great expense.

Still, we had our heroes. Qantas was the world's second airline, founded to service the vast distances of our interior. The very name is an acronym: Queensland and Northern Territory Aerial Services. And there was Kingsford Smith— the first to fly the Pacific, fuel tanks bulging, in a modified American plane. His crossing made Lindbergh's Atlantic feat look like a puddle jump.

Smith and his crew relied on a sextant and sheer will. At one point, they overflew tiny Hawaii in the dark and had to backtrack, low on fuel. They made it to Honolulu on vapors.

My father idolized him. Smith was a man's man, a national icon. For my father's generation, he was what John Lennon would become for mine—an emblem of defiance, possibility, and cultural self-worth.

Leaving Vancouver, we soon wove our way through the gorges and ravines of the Canadian Rockies. Tony and I quickly discovered a spiral staircase that led to a glass "bubble" perched on the roof of one of the carriages. From there, we could take in the breathtaking scenery—so exotic and different from anything we had ever known.

Snow-capped mountains loomed above us, their sides plunging steeply down to valleys far below. Our train threaded through tunnels and glided across towering bridges. The snow shimmered with brilliant white light, dazzling even through the tinted glass— an almost painful glare for our Antipodean eyes. The rivers surged with a youthful, violent energy that made the Darling and Murray seem sluggish and half-hearted by comparison.

Eventually, the Rockies fell behind us, giving way to the endless flatness of the central plains. Where the mountains had been thrilling and strange, the plains were repetitive and dull—a shift from the dress circle to the stalls. The once-mesmerizing view now stretched in monotonous tones of yellow and ochre, wheat fields without end. Tony and I were bored, which, for our parents, meant trouble.

By the time we reached Kansas City for a brief stop, our restlessness must have worn them down. It was decided that we'd disembark and "see a bit of America." Curiously, no one else seemed interested in leaving the train. Fellow passengers watched us with a mix of curiosity and mild alarm. I noticed the glances and whispers but couldn't yet grasp what was so unusual—or inadvisable—about our plans.

We pushed open the carriage door against the force of a merciless wind and stepped out onto the icy platform. The cold was immediate and hostile, as if the air itself meant us harm. It sliced through our layers like steel blades. We were utterly unprepared. The sensation was unlike anything we had experienced—a demonic, unrelenting cold that made Australian winters feel like tea cozies and fireplace chats.

My face ached almost instantly, my lips too numb to speak. Tony clung to his mother's skirt, trying to disappear into its warmth. My father clutched my shoulder as we stumbled back aboard, the heat inside the train enveloping us like a miracle. We practically fell into the carriage, dragging a burst of freezing air behind us, startling the calm of the overheated cabin.

I remember wondering why no one had warned us. Surely they could tell by our accents, our wide-eyed enthusiasm, that we had no idea what we were walking into. But perhaps that's just not how things were done.

We had now learned what "cold" truly meant in the Northern Hemisphere. Australian winters were a rug-over-the-knees kind of affair. This—this was survival.

The state of Kansas sits just above Oklahoma, and soon we arrived in Enid: the small town where we'd begin a new chapter. Its identity was defined by the presence of the U.S. Air Force—without it, Enid might have felt like a cliché of the American South. While not as fiercely conservative as deeper southern states, Oklahoma was still steeped in the legacy of the "Sooners"—settlers who, at the crack of a gun, raced illegally to claim Cherokee land as their own.

It was our first true step into America.

Of course, I knew nothing of this history when we first arrived in Enid. I was just a child living in the first of three houses we would call home during our time there. Our next-door neighbor was Cherokee. For me, he was simply a good friend—someone to climb trees with and share adventures. I was completely ignorant of the racist violence and historical exploitation that underpinned the white success stories of both America and Australia.

We are all, in some way, victims of our time.

I remember the two of us perched at the very top of what felt like a skyscraper-high tree, calling out "Bombs over Tokyo!" while Tony lingered halfway up, unsure whether to climb higher. It had only been fifteen years since the end of World War II, and the echoes of that conflict lingered. In a military family like ours, with a father already considered "a veteran" by American standards, those stories were always close to the surface.

Our first home in Enid was a two-story house with a basement—206 West Cherokee. Tony and I had never encountered a basement before, but it quickly became our refuge from the brutal winter. We'd spend hours downstairs playing cops and robbers or cowboys and Indians. I always cast myself as the good guy—being older, I got to make the rules—but Tony, with his wily charm, almost always managed to flip the story in his favor. That little self-satisfied smile of his said it all.

Tony was still too young for school. I wasn't so lucky. I began at Lincoln Elementary, a formidable two-story brick building that felt more like a fortress than a place of learning. Meanwhile, Tony stayed home and discovered the miracle of American television.

We had first seen color TV on our arrival at Vance Air Force Base, in a mess hall. A wall-mounted screen beamed lurid cartoon colors at us—so bright they seemed to spill out of the box. We were mesmerized, unreachable. It was like gazing through a portal into another world, one with technology that turned walls into magic windows. From that moment on, we were hooked. TV became our drug of choice, a lifelong addiction.

Tony quickly picked up American phrases and accents, learned from endless hours of cartoons and cowboy shows. While I was reciting Bible verses and pledging allegiance at school, Tony was building his American identity through the screen and supermarket aisles. Every supermarket had a vast car park—so large you practically needed a compass to find your car after shopping.

We watched shows like *Rawhide* and *Wagon Train*, which romanticized the lawlessness and violence of the American frontier. The Wild West was repackaged into a myth of brave white cowboys and sneering black-hatted villains. It was a lie, of course, but nations often build themselves on such lies. When Native Americans appeared on screen at all, they existed only to be shot at—an obstacle for white heroes to conquer.

Tony and I rode with Buffalo Bill and Hopalong Cassidy, crossed borders with Pancho and the Cisco Kid. One morning show hosted by Tom Mix ended with what he claimed was a Cherokee farewell gesture: he'd swipe his right arm across his chest and say something that sounded to us like "Washday." We thought it meant he had laundry to do. We laughed for hours over our clever little pun.

Tony's musical ear was starting to show, too. He'd mimic theme songs note for note. One of his favorites was *Rawhide*—he'd belt out the closing line with head tilted back and a thick Aussie twang: "RAAAAwhide!"

My brother spent a lot of time with our mother, and I can't fully account for what passed between them during those early years, but a strong bond formed. I remember years later, when he first started school, Mum found a note he'd left for her during the day: *"I left this because I thought you might be missing me today. I am thinking of you."* My mother never had favorites, but there was something about Tony that mirrored our father—his humor, his manner—that Mum clearly found endearing. Oddly enough, I think she and I clashed more often because I took after her.

I resented the wrench of leaving the warm cocoon of our home each morning to face the bone-deep chill of school. I soon discovered I was considered somewhat exotic in that part of the world, and I learned to lean into it, cultivating a "class clown" persona. At every school, I was the newcomer—disconnected, foreign, and always trying to decode a world that wasn't mine. Humor became my way in. I assumed I was being laughed at, but perhaps it was more that I was laughed *with*. Either way, I didn't mind—as long as I wasn't being ignored or bullied for my differences, I could live with the spotlight, however fleeting.

As cold as it was outside, it was better than being cooped up indoors in those stiflingly overheated American houses. Tony and I would itch to "go outside." Staying in too long gave me headaches. I remember one day vividly: snow piled in drifts high against the windows, sometimes reaching the gutters. We played outside until it reached our waists, our dog bounding after snowballs, re-emerging grinning and ice-coated. He seemed as thrilled as we were to be out in the world. We adored that dog. Leaving him behind in America—thanks to Australia's quarantine rules—was devastating. I still remember the feel of him as a puppy in my hands, still wonder whether someone ever came to collect him from the pound. I hope so. That dog deserved a full, joyful life.

One American Christmas brought with it a Lionel train set—complete with bridges, switches, and a de-coupling mechanism. At first, it was mesmerizing. But no matter how much track we added, the train only ever went in circles. Still, it filled the living room and our imaginations. My father, who had treasured a clockwork Hornby train as a boy, seemed to derive just as much pleasure from it as we did. Thinking back, that train set might be the one place where Tony and I spent the most consistent time with him. For that alone, it was wonderful.

In the backyard of the second house we lived in, during our first American summer, I remember Tony and I wearing Jack Dempsey boxing gloves. Mum wasn't pleased with Dad's purchase—and rightly so. I was older, stronger, and the only opponent available was my younger brother. Tony took more hits than he should have, and I think Mum could see that too clearly. But when we weren't boxing, we wore cowboy chaps and fired off our Fanner Fifties—cap guns that responded to a dramatic sweep of the hand. We were becoming thoroughly Americanized.

Only our return to Australia would reveal how deeply we had absorbed this new identity—how fully we had fallen for the illusion of America as the chosen land, the center of the world, as its television and movies so insistently told us.

Some weeks after our return, when Mum went to relinquish her U.S. driver's license. As the process wrapped up, the bullet-headed American official said, "You must be sad to leave the best country in the world." By now well-accustomed to this sort of arrogant nationalism, Mum replied coolly, "On the contrary—I'm going *back* to the best country in the world."

She said his mouth dropped open. He simply couldn't fathom the possibility that there was somewhere better. Couldn't imagine anything *outside* the borders of his self-appointed paradise.

CHAPTER SIX

Our time in Enid ended as suddenly as it began. Just like that, we were returning to Australia—a place that had become more of an idea than a home. Tony and I had grown up, in many ways, on American soil. The world around us had shaped our imaginations, our routines, and even our language. Everything we knew was American.

We had lived in a world of bikes that looked like cars, with thick white-walled tires, wide handlebars adorned with bells and mirrors, and plastic streamers trailing like fireworks from the ends. There were string ties, rodeos, and the ever-present World Series on television.

The arrival of hi-fi into our living room was momentous. Music poured from huge Magnavox speakers—16-inch woofers, midis, and tweeters—producing a sound so rich it must have echoed across the block. We'd goof off in front of Dad's Bell and Howell Standard 8 movie camera, capturing the kind of family performances now frozen in grainy, flickering memory. Our neighbors had names like Little feather and Running Bear, reminders of another story beneath the surface of American life.

We built snowmen in winters that reached 20 below with the wind chill. Summers sweltered past 100 degrees Fahrenheit. I can still see my father clearing the snow off the path to the car in the morning, his breath misting in the frozen air, hands red with cold as he prepared to drive his 1955 column-shift Ford to work.

Leaving our dog behind—Skippy, a gift from our first American neighbors—was the first grief I remember clearly. We dropped him off at the local pound the day before we left. He was on the top row of cages, looking out. I was in a mood that day, and everyone noticed. But Tony, in his way, tried to comfort Mum, saying, *"Skippy's alright—he got an upstairs apartment."*

There were lazy afternoons at the Vance swimming pool, learning to jump from the one-meter diving board. I remember that exhilarating stillness mid-air, the moment just before the plunge, and then the rush as I broke the surface, that strange, hushed world under water, and the sky blurred and moving above me.

Shopping meant massive brown-paper bags bursting with groceries from supermarkets so huge and full of choice they were almost frightening. Tony and I learned to swim in the nearby Olympic pool, coached by a friendly college student named Bill Sitter. I liked Bill. He had a relaxed warmth and patience that made it easier to push through the nerves.

Tony, though, took coaxing. Despite the heat of the day, he'd complain the water was too cold, too wet, and too *present*. He wasn't weak, just less robust. Until we left for America, he had needed irons to stand upright—so maybe it's not surprising that he hesitated at the water's edge. I was embarrassed sometimes by his poolside antics, not understanding then how far he'd already come. And perhaps the rough waters of the ship pool on the way over had left their own mark.

By the time we left, Tony and I spoke in high-pitched Oklahoma drawls. We didn't realize it until we returned home. But the Americanization ran deep. Tony's use of the word *apartment* was just one clue. We were, for all intents and purposes, little Americans. We looked like them, sounded like them, and understood their world far better than the one we were returning to.

I can clearly remember walking to my first school in Enid, singing "*I Could Have Danced All Night*" from *My Fair Lady*—consciously using the American "danced" with a flat A, instead of my native long A. I could have sung it the way I'd always known, but I didn't. Their "hard A" was not our "hard A," and even though I can't explain the difference precisely, I remember instinctively modifying my accent. I was subtly aware that I was not from here, but I assimilated nonetheless. Survival, even at that age, was tied to fitting in.

A recording still exists of Tony on Fisherman's Wharf in San Francisco—cut onto hot wax at 78 RPM in one of those old booths—while we waited to board the *Oronsay* for our return to Australia. It captures two chirpy, excitable kids with unmistakably American twangs. We even called our father "Sir," an affectation we'd picked up in the States. It sounded proper, respectful—very American.

We didn't know the first thing about Rugby League, cricket, Aussie Rules, meat pies, or mateship.

There was no big send-off when we left Enid. Our parents had to complete some formalities, but for us, it was just another move. We'd already moved house three times in two years. At that stage, Tony and I had a limited awareness of what it meant to be Australian. We were more focused on the excitement of going somewhere new. Now, we were facing the reverse journey. We knew America inside out, and we were heading back to a land that, to us, meant Vegemite and Weet-Bix—two things we craved after years of sugary, cake-like bread and over-sweet everything. What we longed for, without knowing it, was what would later be called "whole food."

The first McDonald's had opened in 1948, and by the time we lived in the U.S., fast-food culture was in full swing. Drive-in diners were everywhere, selling "takeout" in paper sacks. But I don't remember ever eating a hamburger. Our parents didn't approve. They preferred that we eat *food*—real meals, not processed novelty.

Our parents tried to keep Australia alive in us. Their voices alone—so foreign to our newly Americanized ears—were reminders. Adults don't pick up accents like children do, and by the end of our stay, Tony and I thought our parents sounded... strange. Not embarrassingly so, just *different*.

Everything that wasn't packed into boxes was loaded into the Dodge Custom Royal for the drive west. The rest of our belongings were packed into containers—boxes within boxes—destined (hopefully) to arrive in Western Australia months later. I was beginning to grasp just how distressing moving was for my mother. Just as she planted roots, they'd be pulled up again. She became an expert packer, but each move meant hoping for the best and bracing for damage. I can still see her unwrapping chipped trinkets with a kind of silent, weary resignation—guarantees from removalists meant nothing. "Removalist" became a four-letter word in her lexicon.

A table with a broken leg. Smashed crockery. A lounge suite, brand new, arriving with ripped upholstery. These weren't just things—they were part of her sense of stability. The domestic fabric of her life travelled in those boxes. She needed them around her. They were her continuity in an otherwise rootless life.

Every new house meant setting up again. Often, we'd move into homes recently vacated by other Air Force families. Mum dreaded following certain people. The RAAF community was small; paths crossed often. My mother was forensically clean—perhaps unreasonably so—and every new place had to be scrubbed top to bottom before she'd let anything "touch down."

She was left to direct the chaos of removalists and rearrange our lives while juggling two young boys. Tony and I, for our part, found the moving process thrilling. Every new house meant new territory to explore. We even developed our own ritual—we'd race each other to be the first to use the toilet in the new place. I don't know what that says about us, but it became a kind of private tradition, an earthy, sibling way of staking our claim.

Driving across America on smooth turnpikes—glittering silver in the sun—we traversed landscapes as flat as the Hay Plain. Giant towers rose out of nowhere, topped with neon globes announcing food or "restrooms" (never toilets). We stopped at Buckskin Joe's, a Wild West theme park, where Tony and I got to fire a Colt .45. Whether the bell we rang was rigged or not, it felt real to us. In that moment, we earned our notches.

We stayed in motel after motel—identical little worlds with TVs, telephones, and pools. Unbeknownst to us, motels didn't even exist in Australia then. As it happened, one of the passengers we met on the *Oronsay* was studying the "motel phenomenon" to introduce it back home. I think the Flag Inn chain was the outcome of that voyage.

The Dodge was so large that Tony and I could sleep on the back seat with our feet touching. We spent endless miles sprawled across that vast plain, fitfully sleeping, squabbling, and watching the sky roll by. Sometimes, my father would let me sit on his lap and steer the car. I found this both daring and thrilling—pure magic. I don't think my mother ever approved.

At one point on that journey, we were driving between Las Vegas and Los Angeles in the fast lane, where the minimum speed was 80 miles an hour. The Dodge had a red-strip speedometer that glowed from left to right as speed increased. I was perched on my father's lap, Tony's head hanging over the back of the front bench seat—no seatbelts in those days. I vividly remember seeing the speedo hit 105 miles an hour. I could glimpse Tony watching me in the rear-view mirror. I dared not take my eyes off the road for long, but there was a brief moment—just long enough—to catch his smile. His eyes said everything: he understood the thrill I was having. I was steering a right-hand drive car at over a hundred miles an hour. The fighter pilot in me stirred behind my wildly excited eyes.

Then came the Rockies—rising majestically from the plains as we pushed westward toward the coast. Their power hadn't dimmed since we'd last seen them. I remember Bear Lake, feeding Chipmunks in deep snow. We were rugged up for the cold, no longer surprised by it. Life in that part of the northern hemisphere demanded constant adaptation to conditions that could kill you. The chipmunks (which, I imagine, one is no longer encouraged to feed) reminded us of our earliest American experiences. I thought of the freezing Kansas train station that had overwhelmed us on our first arrival. We'd acclimatized. We were, in every sense, Americanized.

San Francisco marked our exit from the U.S. Dad's Dodge had to be loaded onto the *Oronsay*. I can still see him standing anxiously on the wharf as his beloved American icon was hoisted in a sling into the ship's hold. Tony and I stood with him, tracking every slow, swinging inch of that car's journey over the void. Surely, we thought, it would fall—onto the deck, into the sea. But it didn't. The cradle returned empty and silent. No crash. No splash. Only then did Dad exhale and turn his attention back to us—ready to rejoin his family for the long voyage home.

As seasoned shipboard travelers, Tony and I knew what to expect, and to say we were excited would be a colossal understatement. We were vibrating with anticipation—dynamos of unspent energy. Four to five weeks across the Pacific (which was not always pacific) lay ahead, and at the end of it? Weet-Bix and Vegemite. Home.

This time, the voyage seemed to pass faster. I have much clearer memories of the return trip than I do of the journey out. We stopped in Honolulu. It was there, for the first time, that Tony and I became aware of our father's weakness for the female form. We were strolling Waikiki's tourist strip, moving from one shop to another selling muumuus, leis, and all the kitsch Americans thought Hawaiian. In front of us were two young women in bright muumuus. I noticed my father's eyes fixed on their swaying backsides. He saw that I had seen him, and without turning his head, he murmured from the side of his mouth, "They're talking to me, son. They're talking to me." Then, after a pause: "There's yards of it, son—yards of it."

We had lunch beneath the Stevenson tree. I wonder if it's still alive. My memory of that day certainly is.

In Fiji, we watched children dive into the sea near the wharf to retrieve coins thrown by passengers. They scrambled, laughing, through sun-dappled water. It felt like a game, though now I see it for what it was—colonialism's curtain call. Still, in that moment, everyone seemed to be having fun.

We crossed the equator again—this time fully expecting the Neptune ceremony. We were veterans, after all. The ship, slightly larger than the *Orcades*, had a bigger pool, and the crew had organized a swimming carnival for entertainment. There were races, pillow fights on a greasy pole over the pool, and a novelty event involving walking across the same greasy pole and back. Endless skies above. Endless ocean below.

As for the last time I went before Tony, I don't know how the order was determined, but once again, the sea had grown rough, and the pool water slapped violently against its sides. Under gentler conditions, I had completed the greasy pole challenge with skill and ease—too much ease, perhaps. I made it obvious I found it simple, and though I hadn't said a word, my body language boasted. In hindsight, I don't think the others by the pool appreciated it.

Tony stood at the end of the pole, eyeing the churning water and the task ahead. By then, the whole ship was rocking and rolling. He placed one foot on the pole, turned sideways—so

he had to look over his shoulder to see where he was going—
and began to shuffle. One foot forward, a tiny widening of
the gap, then he'd bring the trailing foot up. He moved inch
by inch, an agonizing journey. Eventually, he reached the
other side. Everyone there would've applauded if he had
stepped off then, but no—Tony turned and began the return
trip, as required. Though it had clearly become a death-
defying act to him, he did it. Fear mixed with grit as he crept
back across. When he finally stepped off where he began,
the applause was loud, almost painfully so. What we had
witnessed was raw bravery.

I was so proud of him—and, if I'm honest, vaguely resentful
that he had stolen the limelight once again.

In my defense, I was only eight years old.

That day, Tony showed a courage that would later manifest in
wild, sometimes reckless bravery. I saw something in him—a
stillness, a self-possession, even then. He was braver and
smarter than I was, and I was beginning to understand that.
My only advantage was age: two years and four months more
experience. But I could feel it already—inside his less-than-
sturdy frame was a steady intellect and quiet wisdom. He
was, in many ways, an elder before he was older.

The morning we steamed into Sydney Harbor, Tony and I
had only one thing on our minds: Weet-Bix and Vegemite.
We weren't due to disembark until mid-morning. Breakfast
was being served on board, and while we must have eaten

regularly during the voyage, that morning we made a pact—we'd wait. We wanted *real* breakfast. Australian breakfast. The first in over two years.

We'd been told we wouldn't eat until lunch. Fine by us. Breakfast for lunch? Yes, please. "We'll wait. Thanks, Mum." (Or "Mom," as we still sometimes called her then.)

Sydney felt like a sleepy, water-hugging country town compared to the cities we had seen. Low-rise buildings, tram-track-rippled roads, small cars, and not many people. But it was home. Australia. We were glad to be driving to Roseville.

I don't recall the actual moment Tony and I devoured our long-awaited meal, but I remember us playing in the jacaranda tree at the front of the house—our grandfather's home, shared with two of his daughters.

That night, as always, Tony and I shared a room. The next morning, Aunt Anne told us she'd heard Tony say as he was waking up, "Can you hear the kookaburras, Christopher?"

I don't remember him saying it, but I can hear it now—exactly how he would've said it. How could a four-year-old boy, away from Australia for two years, so keenly identify the call of that bird? It speaks to how embedded place can be in us. How unmistakable, how evocative.

Yes, we were home. But on the wrong side of it.

CHAPTER SEVEN

I was born in August
When the Wattle is in bloom
I must have breathed its perfume
As it came into our room
So, before I can remember
It was a part of me
The golden and the green
What colors this country?
I have lived on foreign shores
Played in waste-deep snow
Been to school in rolled up jeans
It's what I came to know
At six, I'm in America
Where I learned to read and write
When I was first aware of music
Where I first learned wrong from right
But after that adventure
Where next we did alight
The Eucalyptus struck me
And the hard coruscating light
Now, in West Australia

The land of the Kangaroo Paw
It's red and green and yellow
I had never felt before
Wildflowers in the spring
In summer, waiting for the "Doctor."
The relief that it would bring
The cool that it would offer.

From Sydney to Perth was further than we'd ever travelled before. None of us really understood the scale of the undertaking—but we did it in high-tech American style, in Dad's Dodge.

The car itself was a magnet. Wherever we went, it attracted crowds. It was an ostentatious drop-in from the world of Hollywood, dazzling astonished Australian eyes. If we parked to "find a bight to eat"—another of Dad's expressions—or to "ease springs" afterwards, we'd inevitably return to a crowd of onlookers, mouths agape. It was quite the feeling to gently part the gathering, slide into the car, and—like royalty—drive off, all eyes still fixed on us. Our departure was often delayed, as Dad held court with a smile as bright as the Dodge's four-lamp, full-beam headlights blazing.

Unlike America, there were very few towns between cities. Part of the trip took us across the Hay Plain, where we'd stop occasionally to clear the windshield of the smeared remains of insect death. It must have been locust season—at times, the screen darkened with the crushed bodies of these kamikaze grasshoppers.

Like in America, Tony and I would fidget, squirm, argue, try to sleep, laugh at each other's jokes, and generally watch mile after mile of nothing much go by.

Our first major stop was Port Pirie, South Australia, where the Dodge was loaded onto a train, and we were too, bound for Perth via the Nullarbor. (What a bore—not a boar. Hardly a tree, not a hill, naught but naught.) We arrived in Perth in the middle of summer.

We had gone from the depths of an American winter to the peak of an Australian summer in six weeks—literally from one side of the planet to the other. From slow Southern drawls to nasal Australian twangs. From a town called Enid to one called Bullsbrook. The only thing they had in common was a nearby military base. Otherwise, neither had much going for them. These communities—and many others we would live in—existed in a love-hate relationship with the Air Force. They owed their vibrancy to it, but resented the fly-in-fly-out nature of military life. It was modernism meeting small-town inertia.

That Western Australian summer is when Tony started to emerge, physically. The air, the sun, the outdoors—it all seemed to awaken something in him. He became increasingly athletic, in a sadly clumsy way. Will replaced talent. But if he wanted to swim properly, kick a ball, sidestep, or catch a high football, he would apply himself with relentless determination.

Our upstairs married quarters were airy and bright. Sun poured in from every angle—a stark contrast to the last two years. Yes, America has summers, but not like this. The sun here was ferocious. That year, we discovered the agonizing joy of sunburn—though nothing like what was to come once the Olympic-sized pool was installed just down the road.

I loved going barefoot, but sometimes the heat made it impossible to cross a tarred road. By late afternoon, the melted bitumen would bubble and blister. Running across it meant fusing parts of your soles to the road. It was excruciating—unless you were nimble and fast.

Still, we loved this wide-open, hot place.

Going to school was a joy. We'd walk a narrow bush track, marveling at the smells—especially the gum trees. I loved how light danced on the long, grey-green leaves. In spring, wildflowers exploded in dazzling colors, leaping from the inhospitable soil like nature's fireworks. They bloomed briefly, then retreated, exhausted by their own effort. Most of the year, they were anonymous twigs. But spring was their party—life's reward for enduring.

It was Tony's first experience of school. He took to it exactly as I imagined he would. That is to say, without drama. He wasn't blindly compliant or lacking in spirit, but he understood what was expected and got on with it—unlike his histrionic older brother.

Around this time, I began to see both my brother and the world more clearly—literally. I told my parents I couldn't read the blackboard from the back of the classroom. A visit to the optometrist revealed significant myopia.

When I put on glasses for the first time, I was astounded. (I've since seen videos of people hearing for the first time with a cochlear implant—that's what it felt like.) The world had edges. Trees had leaves and branches—I could see them *without* walking up close. It was a revelation.

I was an active kid, so glasses were a nuisance. I went through many pairs, usually smashing them off my face doing energetic boy things. Still, I was grateful for the life-changing clarity. I began to wonder what else might be wrong with me that could be corrected by a prescription.

Apparently, I once told my mother, "I didn't know there wasn't two of everything."

She felt immense guilt—for having left me, metaphorically, in the dark for eight years. But even then, I didn't see it as her fault. How could she have known? *I* didn't know. I thought everyone saw the world the way I did.

My parents, in their own ways, always did the best they could for their "two boys."

One Christmas, we were told to "go and play outside"—and not to return until the whistle. That whistle was how Dad summoned us home at the end of each day. As usual, we did as we were told and ended up in the enclosed courtyard behind the block of flats. But nothing much was happening, and we grew bored.

"I think we should go back upstairs," I said. Tony hesitated. "But we were told not to." I pushed. I won.

We crept up the back stairs and found the house empty—until we discovered our parents in our bedroom, assembling our Christmas present. Matching curtains and bedspreads. They looked up as we entered, and the disappointment on Dad's face was unmistakable. I had done the wrong thing. I knew it the instant I stepped through the doorway.

We helped them finish, but the moment had been lost. The surprise—gone. I felt guilty. Not for the last time, I wished I had listened to Tony.

The bedspreads and curtains were a celebration of American railroads: meters of trains chugging toward destinations like Santa Fe and Chicago. I suppose Mum and Dad were referencing our Lionel train set or our recent American rail travel. Still, I remember thinking it was all oddly placed—slightly foreign, somehow. Perhaps it felt incongruous with the plain walls of an Australian child's bedroom. Strange, how quickly we were becoming "home."

I don't recall winter in Perth. What I do remember are dry, blisteringly hot days that began with the sun and seemed to go on forever, even after it dipped behind the horizon. We spent our days longing for the arrival of the

"Fremantle Doctor," the coastal breeze that swept up from Fremantle into Pearce, as if someone had switched on the air conditioning around three-thirty every afternoon. It brought instant relief—cooling our sweat-soaked skin, dropping the temperature by degrees. Yet to outsiders, that "relief" would still have felt like a furnace.

At night, we lay drenched in sweat, longing for the breeze to linger. Summer offered little mercy.

That first summer at Pearce, the new Olympic-sized pool became the rhythm of our days. Mornings at the pool. Lunch. The ritual hour-long wait after eating. Then back to the pool until sunburnt, exhausted, and ready to collapse into bed. Overnight, we'd recover—barely—in time to do it all again.

Tony began to find his element in the water. He still wasn't a strong swimmer and belly-flopped rather than dived, splay-legged and graceless. But he grew confident—confident in a way I hadn't seen before. Gone was the shivering child from Enid, crouched poolside in fear, arms crossed tightly over his chest. This was a new version of Tony—engaged, active, willing. He wasn't born into health like I had been; he was building his through sheer will.

I didn't recognize it then, but this was one of the earliest signs of a truth that would define his too-short life: a quiet, dogged determination to *do well what you do*—no matter how difficult, no matter how long it took.

At this stage, we lived our lives *together*, but not always *with* each other. Tony often played alone, fully absorbed in his own world. He'd create entire universes in his mind, and when I interrupted—accidentally or not—he'd "look up" slowly, taking time to recalibrate and return to reality. I envied that capacity. I needed external stimulus. Tony had everything he needed inside him.

Religion—Presbyterian, to be precise—was still a significant part of our lives. We were part of the high church tradition, the Scottish end, and our mother remained deeply steeped in its rituals. My father, raised Catholic, had relinquished any role in our religious upbringing, much to the disbelief—and anger—of his family when he married.

One Sunday morning, as we walked to Sunday school, Tony and I flanking our mother, I looked up and asked, "If you had to choose between Tony and me and Daddy, who would you choose?"

Tony heard the question and, like me, waited for the answer.

Without a moment's hesitation, she replied, "Oh, your father, of course."

We walked on. Tony and I looked at each other, stunned. Her answer had come as casually as if I'd asked what time it was or whether the sun was up. There was no doubt in her voice—but I minded. I really minded. That moment stays hard in my memory.

Still, those days in Western Australia were among the best of my life—days of bronzed freedom, constant sunshine, and endless school holidays. Cricket, Aussie rules, the sounds of our parents playing tennis on the base courts. We both had to tiptoe around the house on Saturday mornings so as not to "wake your father," recovering from the Friday night Mess—a drunken ritual passed down by his generation from the war.

Occasionally, Dad took us to watch Swan Districts play South Fremantle at a suburban ground. But the heart of those years was the pool: long, languid, sun-drenched days spent swimming, diving, lazing under the blinding West Australian sky.

But the idyll didn't last. Dad was posted to the Staff College in Canberra. We moved in late 1962.

By then, Tony and I were weary of the constant upheaval. We never truly settled. Just as friendships began to solidify, we'd be uprooted. I was briefly "leader of the pack," but I was learning not to commit—to hold back.

David Cutler was my first best friend. Nicholas Elliott ran a close second. David and I founded the 333 Club, where I insisted the backward "3" was correct for our clubhouse sign. He disagreed but let it be. Later, I realized he was right. That sign became a silent "I told you so."

He was the first person—apart from Tony—with whom I conspired against the world. I suppose I loved him in a child's way. I wouldn't have thought in those terms then—and hadn't until writing this now—but leaving Perth meant letting go of David. That loss taught me something lasting: that life, for us, would always be impermanent. Wherever we were, where we'd been no longer mattered. A new posting meant a new version of ourselves.

We became different people in different places, and that fragmentation made it hard to see who we really were.

Tony, being younger, may not have made such deep attachments yet. But even for him, each move was a strange combination of excitement and regret—looking forward to new possibilities while mourning what we left behind.

We loved it. We hated it. But it was the only life we knew.

An enervating, elevating adventure.

We were both lucky—and cursed.

CHAPTER EIGHT

One day, while we were still in Western Australia, Dad drove into Perth and came back with a brand-new push-button automatic Valiant and £1,000 in his pocket. Although he seemed pleased to have a new car, there was no denying that—despite his insistence—it didn't fully meet his expectations. He did, however, like the novelty of the push-button automatic, and so did Tony and I. To us, it was the height of sophistication.

The car was emerald green, Australian-built, and modest compared to the Dodge. It would be our transport back to the Eastern States. Australians instinctively knew American cars wouldn't survive long without local adaptation. We knew better—we'd driven the Dodge across all kinds of terrain. It might have been ostentatious, a "living room on wheels," but it had grit. Still, this Valiant, though smaller and less grand, was more suited to "Australian conditions"—by which we meant the heat, dust, and inadequate roads.

Tony and I found its practical size a relief; it parked easily, moved through narrow streets, and didn't attract gawking strangers. Gone were the days of returning to the car to find a crowd gathered around the Dodge. The Valiant was anonymous. Functional. A step down, but a logical one.

When we bought it, we were suspended between memories of America and the journey to come. Our plan was to drive to Kalgoorlie—a gold rush town where every corner once boasted a pub—and from there, put the car on a train to cross the vast, sandy belly of the continent.

Leaving Pearce followed the usual pattern: packing up, watching the truck drive away with our belongings, and hoping it would eventually reintroduce us to ourselves at the new house.

The long drive with Tony, who had now revealed a worrying tendency toward car sickness, was less than thrilling. We all learned to spot the signs: silence from the normally chatty Tony, a sudden pallor, that hunted-animal glance as he searched desperately for an escape. Without a word, we'd all sense it—the ominous stillness—and brace for what came next: the retching, the awful smell, the stink that clung to everything.

Sometimes we were fast enough to act in time. Other times, we weren't. Then we'd drive for miles with windows down, the air heavy with vinegar-laced regret. I'd hang my head out the window, whining about how awful it was. Mum would dry-retch as she wiped down the back of the seat. I don't remember Dad ever helping with cleanup. It would've been

Ironic if the fighter pilot didn't have the stomach for it. I certainly didn't—but I was just a kid, trapped in a travelling vomitorium.

Of course, I still loved my brother. But I sometimes wished he could keep his meals to himself. The car filled with not just stench, but his embarrassment. No one found it funny—not even Tony.

He had a sweet tooth, too—one that rivalled his sensitivity to motion. Mum made Pavlova for his birthdays, a sticky mess that made my teeth ache just looking at it. He devoured it with machine-like fervour. For me, she made apple pie—no sugar, no cinnamon. Real pie eaters would've called it boring. I called it perfect. I still eat the occasional apple pie now, but Sara's is too sweet, and Nana's isn't quite like Mum's.

Dad did most of the driving, of course. That was the way of things: men drove; women didn't. Tony and I sat in the back, squabbling and squirming, farting and fighting as the miles rolled by. It was as though we each had our designated in-car roles.

We played "Spotto," "I Spy" (or "Eye Spy?"), counted black cows versus brown cows, and watched out for specific makes of car. I always cheered for the Valiant, though Tony knew better—he backed the Falcon or the Holden. Holden always won. Still, I stayed loyal to the underdog Chrysler. It was like rooting for your footy team or defending Norm O'Neill's batting average. Loyalty trumped logic.

I invented another game: making up words using the letters on license plates—in order. My two-year age advantage gave me a stronger vocabulary, but Tony was catching up. Compared to our parents in the front seat—Dad with his Shakespeare, Mum quoting Dickens—we were amateurs. But we held our own. Besides, Dad was driving, and Mum was navigating.

Somewhere between nowhere and Coolgardie, Mum suggested she take over the wheel. Dad, somewhat reluctantly, agreed. Not long after, the car began losing power. We'd heard the murmurs in the front seat—muffled speculation about what was wrong. Finally, the Valiant gave up entirely. We were stranded in the middle of the Western Australian outback, thirty miles from Coolgardie.

We had passed signs—roughly painted and nailed to trees—advertising "Jack's Motel" as the weary traveler's salvation. That had been our destination, and Tony and I were hoping for an American-style end-of-day payoff: pool, TV, playground.

Instead, we stood on the roadside beside a limp green car, staring at a trail of transmission fluid stretching behind us as far as the eye could see. At least we knew what the problem was. And to Mum's relief, it had nothing to do with her driving.

After what felt like days of emptiness, a car finally appeared on the horizon—a beat-up old VW Beetle, the first vehicle we'd seen in hours. It slowed, coughed to a stop, and out stepped two men I could only describe as bush-bound throwbacks. They wore blue singlets, dusty jeans, and an air of the unexpected.

"Need help?" they asked. My parents hesitated.

Something about them made us uneasy. There was politeness in their tone, but wariness in our father's stance. We could feel the tension between our parents—unsure whether this chance encounter was salvation or danger. The vastness around us made our vulnerability painfully clear.

Conversation followed, clipped and cautious. It wasn't long before we noticed the rifles in their car. One of the men offered to show them to Tony and me. My parents politely declined. The offer persisted. Before long, we were holding them—heavy, cold, and utterly foreign. The men laughed, firing shots into the bush as we stood nearby, stunned and silent.

Mum looked horrified. Her fear radiated through the dry air. But then, as quickly as they'd appeared, the men returned to their car, promising to alert the owner of Jack's Motel— who also doubled as the local NRMA or whatever Western Australia called its roadside service. They'd send him back to tow us into Coolgardie.

Relief flooded Mum's face the moment the VW disappeared into the heat haze. Still, we were alone again, swallowed by the vast, indifferent bush. Dad, deciding to be useful— or to keep us occupied—suggested lighting a fire so Jack could find us more easily. It seemed logical at the time. Only now do I wonder why we thought a fire was necessary, considering our precise location was now in the hands of two gun-toting strangers, and there was only one road in or out.

But Dad needed to *do* something. We collected dry twigs, larger sticks, and branches. He built the fire meticulously, stacking it like a miniature fortress. A smoker in those days, he struck a match and lit the base. The flames leapt up instantly—greedy and wild, fueled by tinder-dry wood.

Then the wind rose.

The clearing narrowed into a corridor of gum trees. The fire jumped. Sparks flew. Suddenly, the bush to one side was alight.

It was the closest we'd seen to our father panicking. There was an urgency in his movements, not quite fear—but close. He shouted at us to grab branches, to beat the fire out. We did—wildly, desperately, afraid we were about to burn down half of Western Australia.

Luckily, the wind died down as quickly as it had arrived. The flames receded. We stood, blackened and breathless, before a scorched patch of earth—a harsh reminder of how easily control slips away.

By the time dusk crept over the trees, Jack had yet to appear. I can't remember how we passed the time—maybe Tony and

I played hopscotch or made up silly games—but eventually, a battered Ute pulled up, and Jack introduced himself with a brief nod. He connected a tow rope between our car and his Ute, and before we could settle in, we were racing toward Coolgardie at an alarming speed.

Dad muttered angrily that the rope was too short. "I won't have time to react if he stops suddenly," he snapped. The tension inside the car was thick. We could feel it: Dad was afraid. And if he was afraid—this man who had flown jets and faced combat—then something *must* be wrong.

We sat in silence, clutching the seats as the Coolgardie lights finally shimmered into view.

An hour later, we arrived. The car would be fixed overnight. Jack, now our host, guided us to "Jack's Motel." Tony and I stared in disbelief.

This wasn't a motel. It was a collection of corrugated iron sheds—maybe three or four. No pool, no TV, no air-conditioning. No comfort. More like barns than bedrooms. They looked like places you'd store hay, not sleep in.

Tony looked at me. I looked at him. We didn't say a word. We didn't need to.

Tony and I were thirsty. Against one of the sheds at "Jack's Motel," I spotted a tap. We hurried over, hopeful. Tony twisted the handle, and after an eternity of rusty groans, a thin trickle sputtered out—along with a startled redback spider doing a panicked backstroke in my cupped hands.

We leapt away.

"You nearly swallowed a redback," Tony said, half-laughing, half-appalled.

He was right. We stayed thirsty.

I don't remember much of that night in the "motel," but the next day we were on the road again, heading for Kalgoorlie to rendezvous with the train that would take us—along with our Valiant—back across the Nullarbor.

That night, Tony and I were given a room of our own in an old hotel with a wrought-iron balcony that felt like something from a different, more elegant world. The bathroom was at the end of the hall, and our parents' room was far away—much to Mum's dismay and our delight. We were giddy with the idea of independence, dreaming of mischief. Nothing came of it, of course.

Soon enough, the car was loaded onto the flatbed car behind the passenger train, and we settled in for the long return journey. We'd already decided that "Nullarbor" was short for "null bore"—and the second crossing only confirmed that impression. Endless plains. Treeless. Lifeless. Tedious beyond imagining for a ten-year-old.

We were relieved when the car was finally offloaded in Port Pirie. We resumed our road journey through the South Australian outback, across the bug-splattered Hay Plain, and finally arrived at Lawley House—our temporary accommodation in a weathered old suburb of Canberra.

The next day we went to inspect "the new house."

What a disaster.

It was a first-generation Canberra "government house"—low-slung, hunched under oversized European trees, with all the charm of a half-buried bunker. The moment we opened the front door, the stench hit us like a wave—putrid, like rotting meat. Mum gagged and took a step back.

"Nothing goes in here until I've cleaned it. I don't care if we have to delay the removalists," she said firmly. She was furious—and rightly so.

Dad, already tense from his new posting, didn't need this. He would be staying at Fairbairn Base during his Staff Course, and now he had a distraught wife and two children housed in squalor. But he didn't argue. He knew she was right.

We walked through the place. It was dark, depressing. The toilet reeked of old urine. The kitchen walls were slick with years of baked-in grease. The carpets—if you could call them that—were shredded, threadbare, and dotted with holes.

Then Mum called Dad over. Wordlessly, she pointed to the carpet outside the bathroom. He looked down. Maggots.

Tiny, white, writhing creatures crawling out from beneath the carpet and onto the linoleum floor.

That was the final straw. Dad turned to us and said something along the lines of, "This is unacceptable." And we left.

We stayed at Lawley House for another week until we finally moved into 25 McCaughey Street, Turner. We were there for about a year, unhappily, before my parents made a decision—they would build their first real home.

It was then I began to realize that my father, for all his capability in military service, was a novice in the civilian world. He believed in a system where orders were followed, promises meant something, and people were held to account. But the private sector was nothing like that. There were no guarantees—just deals and half-truths and shifting commitments.

So when they hired a builder—who turned out to be a con artist—it was no surprise that things went awry. They were scammed. Delayed. Taken for fools. Only by sheer luck, not planning, did they finally move into their new brick-veneer home on Ferdinand Street in Campbell.

Dad named it *El Casa Toro*, tipping his hat to the street's Spanish name. It was supposed to be a new beginning.

Maybe it was.

But it came at the end of a long, strange journey through the outback, the bureaucracy, and the brutal reality of civilian life.

CHAPTER NINE

We must have arrived in Canberra during the school holidays, because moving into the Turner house and enrolling at Turner Primary School happened almost simultaneously. Our previous home—Bullsbrook—had a name that practically invited mockery. It sounded like the kind of place where cousins married and cows outsmarted people. So when our school records were transferred, our new headmaster, Mr Betts, met our academic histories with a smirk of disbelief.

Despite being placed in the top classes wherever we'd been, Mr Betts clearly regarded our achievements with suspicion. My mother, never one to back down, firmly stated that both her boys were intelligent and their records deserved respect. Mr Betts—small in both stature and, as it turned out, intellectual generosity—looked at her and said, "But you're in Canberra now, dear. This school is full of the children of doctors, lawyers, and diplomats."

My mother probably said something like "So what?" though I'm sure she was biting back a far more pointed reply. She demanded her children be placed according to merit, not postcode.

To resolve the issue, Mr Betts devised a placement test. We each sat for it, answering questions appropriate to our age groups. I was placed in 6A—the top class. Tony, inexplicably, was dumped into 4C, the lowest. This didn't sit well with any of us.

While I was always considered the athlete and Tony the aesthete, it had never been implied that either of us lacked brains. But to place Tony, of all people, in the lowest stream? My mother knew something was wrong.

With Dad busy saving the free world from communism or whatever threat America had deemed pressing at the time, Mum took up the fight herself. She made an appointment with Mr Betts and sat across from him as he laid out our test papers. "Your eldest did well," he admitted, "but your second boy didn't even finish his test."

Mum took one look at Tony's paper, recognized his large, looping handwriting, and asked Mr Betts to kindly turn the page over.

On the back: the rest of the answers.

Evidently, no one in the faculty of Canberra's children-of-diplomats had thought to check if a ten-year-old had continued his work on the other side of the paper. Betts looked sheepish. Tony was moved to the class that matched his ability.

That encounter crystallized something for me: my growing mistrust of authority figures. Mum said later, "Why are the children of doctors and lawyers inherently smarter than the children of a pilot?" Mr Betts never answered.

If Canberra was meant to be the intellectual capital of the country, we'd seen no proof. Just the same small-town arrogance, only dressed in blazers and clipped vowels.

On my first day in 6A, Mr Betts escorted me to class. As we entered, a voice chirped, "Hey, four-eyes."

Nice, I thought. Charming welcome.

Mr Bourke, the teacher, practically sprang out of his chair to let Betts sit behind the desk. Betts took the seat, looked me up and down, and barked, "You'll have to work like a tiger to stay in this class."

At the time, it struck me as harsh. If I really was the dunce he seemed to think I was, perhaps I didn't belong there at all.

The next day, seating arrangements were determined by a maths test—arithmetic, as it was probably still called then. The top scorers sat in the front right-hand corner of the room, the lowest scorers in the back left. That's where I ended up: academic Siberia. The front corner felt as distant as Bullsbrook. Maths had never been my strength. Had the seating been based on English, composition, or comprehension, I'd have been much closer to the front.

Still, Mr Betts's words echoed in my head: "You'll have to work like a tiger to stay in this class." At that point, I didn't feel like a tiger. I felt like a tabby. And I started to believe he might be right. I could almost feel myself slipping down the academic pole, and it unsettled me more than I expected.

Meanwhile, Tony was likely handling 4A with his usual quiet brilliance. We didn't talk about school much—actually, we were starting to drift apart. He had begun to find his own friends, and I wasn't sure how I felt about it. Part of me missed him wanting to tag along. But another part of me found his company a liability, especially in sport. He was clumsy, uncoordinated, always the last one picked. I had often chosen him only because he was my brother and I couldn't bear to leave him standing there, head bowed and humiliated. But having Tony on the team meant starting a game a step behind.

That said, I still cherished our early days in Canberra, before school and social groups got in the way. Our house in Turner sat across from one of Canberra's many concrete-lined creeks—Sullivan's Creek. Its sloped edges formed perfect riding ramps, and a mossy trickle of water always ran down the center. If you hit it straight, you could cross to the other side cleanly. Hit it wrong, and you'd slide out in a soggy, graceless heap.

We used to ride for miles like that, discovering our new world. Canberra's backyards rolled past us like the private scenes glimpsed from a train window—unguarded, exposed. We carved our initials into a tree across from our house. Years later, when I returned, I went to look for it. The tree was still there, but the carving was gone.

That, too, felt like something lost.

Another cherished memory is the morning Tony and I climbed Mt Ainslie behind our house in Campbell. We rose in near-darkness and set off up what must have been an old, long-forgotten access track—steep, direct, and demanding. As we ascended, the mist clung to us like breath on glass. By the time we reached the summit, the world below had vanished under a blanket of fog.

It was eerily quiet. The city hadn't yet stirred. No tourists, no distractions—just Tony, me, and the first tentative birdsong of morning. As we stood there talking, the mist began to lift, revealing Canberra beneath us, catching the early sun in flashes of chrome. We didn't say anything about it, but we both knew: this moment was ours alone.

We smiled at each other, completely in the moment. Life was good that morning. I was with the best person I knew, and he was my brother. It was then that we silently recognized a truth that would hold across years and distance—we would always be there for each other. The bond wasn't made that day; it was revealed.

Tony was the best and worst thing that happened to me.

Another day, we rode across town to Black Mountain, pedaled to the top, and came down again as fast as our rattling frames would carry us. No helmets. No traffic to worry about. Just the wind in our faces and eyes watering from the speed. Had we fallen, it would have meant broken bones—or worse—but we were kids, wild and free in a Canberra still more sheep paddock than capital.

Later, we found ourselves circling the King O'Malley foundation stone atop Capitol Hill, looking out over the empty basin that would become Lake Burley Griffin. Back then, Canberra still felt like a country town with grand ambitions.

That hill now lies beneath the Parliament House that squats over the city like a landed spacecraft. I wonder where the stone is now.

As I said, our earliest days in Canberra were spent in Turner. And in the strange, complex arena of a new school, it was sport—or foolishness—that seemed to offer a way in. I trialed for the cricket team. I was bowling well, and I could hear the approving murmurs from the coaches. I had no idea this would be the last day I'd ever play the game.

What happened next doesn't need retelling here—this is my story with Tony. But the accident left me physically marked and visibly changed for over a year. My two front teeth were gone, left in the forehead of another boy as we both leapt for the same catch.

I became a joke—and so, I became the joker. I leaned into it, trying to survive until we moved to Campbell and I started anew.

At Campbell Primary, I tried again. I told myself I still wanted to play cricket. But minutes into the tryouts, a ball fell from the sky like a missile, and I misjudged it. It struck me square in the forehead, leaving a rising lump so large and stitched with the seam of the ball that even an emu might have been proud. That was it for me and cricket—and for team sports entirely, except for a short-lived Rugby League stint at the end of school.

Before all that, back in the West, Dad had taken up a new obsession: golf.

> *God give me the round due to me*
> *And I'll get down on bended knees*
> *I'd pay due penance*
> *Just for the one chance*
> *To be free of mediocrity*
> *I used to practice three days a week*
> *Until my swing was so sweet*
> *But on the course, it collapses, of course*
> *Still the same old me*
> *It wasn't warm-hearted, but I was eight*
> *When I first saw my father irate*

He missed the shortest of puts
It looked like he'd been punched in the guts
And I just stared
Over the years, I tried to concentrate
But at that, I am so second-rate
I should swing round my head
I move it instead
And the ball goes anywhere

As mentioned in the song, I was eight the first time I went to a golf course with my father. From the first tee, he sliced his drive into a small copse of trees. He strode off—only a short walk—and disappeared among the trunks. From within came a flurry of "swishing" sounds, which I now know where the unmistakable sighs of an air swing. Then, the ball, humbled and wobbling, bounced a few meters back toward the fairway. His club followed, helicoptering after it, and in fact went farther than the ball itself.

My father emerged looking sheepish, and we continued in silence. On the green, he missed a short putt and cast a glare at me as though I'd nudged the ball away with my mind. I should have known then that this game was no more suited to me than it was to him.

And yet, fifty years later, I still mumble and bumble my way around golf courses, eternally ungraceful. The game has caused me more frustration and humiliation than it ever has pleasure. These days, it's just exercise—and a test of my ability to laugh at myself.

Tony, wisely, didn't take to golf. A moment that sealed it came one day at Federal Golf Club, on the thirteenth hole. Tony, our mother, and I were there together. I hit a less-than-stellar shot—though to me, anything that didn't land in the center of the fairway, green, or hole was unacceptable. In frustration, I flung my three-iron—purchased from the David Jones store in Parramatta—down before me. It bounced. The butt of the grip sprang back and smashed my glasses from my face. They lay broken at my feet, along with my self-respect.

I felt, in that moment, how my father must have felt all those years ago. Humiliated. Exposed.

Tony looked at me with something between disbelief and pity. He turned to our equally stunned mother and said, "I'll never play this game after seeing what it does to Christopher."

And he didn't.

Which was a shame in some ways—he had a naturally fluid, wristy swing (albeit with a tendency to slice) that, with a bit of guidance, could have been shaped into something rather good. And with his calm, composed personality, he might have made a fine golfer.

But he was smart enough not to let the game ruin him like it did me.

****

We went to Turner Primary and later to Campbell Primary during our time in Canberra. I then attended Canberra High School for a year before transferring to the newly built Campbell High. Tony, still in primary school, had a different daily rhythm. But most days ended the same way: our family gathered around the flickering "twenty-three"—a twenty-three-inch black-and-white television—eating our evening meal. The tradition of sitting at the dinner table had long since faded. Like many families of the time, we had fallen under the spell of this miraculous box of moving images.

We even had a choice of channels—ABC or Channel 7, from memory. But we were an ABC family. Without fail, we watched the 7 PM news each night. Tony and I would have loved to sample the "commercial TV," but my father made it clear: we did not watch that. At school the next day, other kids would talk about what they'd seen on those commercial stations, and Tony and I could only smile blankly. Still, we had our own rituals: *This Day Tonight* and the Monday night fixture, *Four Corners*, whose theme music Tony and I loved.

In truth, my father and Tony were the funny ones in the family. I often envied their quick wit. I was usually just behind the beat—close, but not quite. I was frequently the target of their good-natured teasing, and I wore that role with a mix of frustration and affection.

But one night, as we were watching the news, I had my moment.

Andrew Swanton was reporting on something fairly unremarkable when I said, apropos of nothing, "He should be called Butpaint Duck Hundredweight."

"What?" my father asked.

"Butpaint Duck Hundredweight. It makes as much sense as Andrew Swanton."

There was a moment of hesitation. Then—laughter. Real laughter. They howled. For the first time, they looked at me not as the punchline, but as the source of the joke. Had they underestimated me? Was I—maybe, just maybe—as funny as they were?

The sports segment came on. Ken Rosewall's name popped up, and I—riding the wave—asked, "Ken Rosewall could equally be known as Ken Petunia Partition".

They burst out laughing again. That night, I felt I'd been admitted into a club. The Club of the Quick-Witted. A club where cleverness was currency, and wit was the measure of your worth.

I lived in fear of not being able to follow it up.

I never did. But that night, I was front and centre. That night, I was funny. And I'll never forget it.

****

By now, we were living in Campbell. Tony was still at Campbell Primary; I was at Campbell High. Because we went to different schools, we lived increasingly separate lives. We'd see each other at the start and end of the day—he would go off and do whatever little brothers did, and I would get on with the awkward process of transitioning to yet another school. At least this time, I was doing it alongside classmates from Canberra High, temporarily housed there while Campbell High was under construction.

Tony was growing up and beginning to define himself outside the family. We had distinct social circles. His friends seemed sharper, funnier, more interesting than mine. I understood why—Tony was effortlessly charismatic. I resented it at times, the ease with which people were drawn to him. Soon, his guitar playing would only amplify this.

It started with him pestering Dad for a drum kit. Instead, he got a cheap, hard-to-play electric guitar—the kind where the action is so high it demands strong, determined hands. Dad, flying missions in and out of Southeast Asia—often transporting the grim cargo of body bags filled with the fallen flower of Australian youth—brought back a small valve amplifier. That amp became part of Tony's bedroom landscape.

He took to the guitar like a conservative to ignorance. It was as though the instrument had been waiting for him to find it. This was the era of the British Invasion, the golden age of The Beatles and the birth of English rock. Everyone knew John,

Paul, George, and Ringo. The air was alive with new, melodic energy. Music was evolving—no longer in short pants, but stepping boldly into the avant-garde.

We were hooked. Beatles posters covered our walls. Around this time, Dad returned from Asia with the first transistor radios—small, portable, personal. For our generation, the transistor was the internet. It liberated us. That little black box pumped music and meaning into our lives.

I didn't "get" Elvis until Lennon said, "Before Elvis, there was nothing." Then I listened to early Elvis and understood what Lennon had heard. It came through him, and into me.

The first time Tony and I heard *She Loves You* was at Dad's urging. He was outside weeding when he burst in, breathless: "Boys, you have to hear this!" He loved music and was the first person we knew who was into the Beatles. "Listen to the backbeat," he said. "This is the future of music."

That song changed our lives. We stared at the radio in disbelief, stunned by the energy pouring out of it. That first ecstatic chorus was transcendent. I've been chasing that feeling ever since. The music you hear in your youth lives forever in your soul. I've loved music ever since, but nothing has ever moved me the way *She Loves You* did in that moment.

We never got back on the rails after that. We missed many trains, slept through many stations, but we didn't care—we lived in Music Land, and everything else felt mundane and off-track.

One day, I saw a copy of *Please Please Me* strapped to the back of someone's bike at school. I ached to hold it, to slide the vinyl onto Dad's hi-fi and hear it through his Magnavox speakers. It was a world within reach, but just out of grasp. The door to our bedroom was on his side of the room. He looked toward the door and then said, "OK I agree this is my side and that is yours and I respect the fact that you don't want me on your side of the line. Equally I don't want you on my side of the line which means that you are going to starve to death. How are you going to get in and out of the room? Curses foiled again.

I told Tony that night. We agreed to save our pocket money—LPs cost 52 shillings and 6 pence. No sense buying the same one, so I'd get *Please Please Me*, and he'd get *With the Beatles*. When we had the money, Mum took us to the record bar at David Jones in the new Monaro Mall. In the following weeks, we wore those records out.

One day, *Please Please Me* was blasting from the speakers. It was so loud Mum had to shout, "Does it have to be so loud?" Tony, pounding his chest with joy, shouted back, "If it doesn't hit you in the chest, it's not worth listening to." I grinned in agreement, as wide as the living room we danced in.

I didn't take up the guitar then. I wish I had—those are the formative years when learning sticks like nothing else. When I finally picked it up at nineteen, taught some chords by a uni friend, I was always going to be behind. Tony was already on his way.

So, no matter how I try
I'll never play as well as you
No matter how well I sing
I'll never sing as you used to
So why do I try,
Keep walking down that path
When I know I will not arrive
While you are in my past
I'm lonely
Lonely without you

Why didn't I take up the guitar in those early Campbell years? I knew exactly what Tony was doing—I saw his progress—but I didn't yet feel the need to *articulate* music. That would come later. What we did share, however, was a deep, unshakable adoration for the best of English rock, and increasingly, for the Indigenous sound embodied most powerfully by the Easybeats. Yes, they were a transported English band, but for us, they were ours. We used to say that if the Easies had taken off in the UK after peaking in Australia, they'd have been as big as The Who, The Kinks, or The Stones. To us, they were the only band—Australian or otherwise—that came close to the Beatles. And there was no greater compliment.

I would have fallen completely under their spell if Little Stevie had been a better singer. But in time, I came to understand something else: Lennon and McCartney were *great* singers who wrote *great* songs. That combination has never been remotely matched.

We always had each other.

Some days, Tony was in the way—too slow, not strong enough, or not athletic enough. But mostly, being with him made life lighter. I can still see us walking beneath the tall gums of Treloar Crescent, behind the Australian War Memorial, whose sprawling grounds fed our imaginations for hours. He was often smiling, often laughing. He was the most positive of people, and I cherished the times he chose to hang out with me rather than with his clever, fast-talking friends.

He could always make me laugh. And I loved making him laugh. There was a specific joy in seeing his face register the humour in something I'd said—then hearing that burst of laughter as he threw back his head and looked at me, amused and slightly astonished. That look meant everything. Making my father and brother laugh is still one of the great joys of my life. They made me laugh so easily; returning the favour felt like magic.

Behind the War Memorial, a de facto path snaked into the low rise of Mount Ainslie. We watched other kids take billy carts to the hill and race down it, and we decided to join them. Over two weekends, we built our own—a sleek machine we considered the Rolls Royce of billy carts. It was state-of-the-art, and we wheeled it to the end of the street and into the paddock, proud as punch.

The slope looked manageable from a distance, but up close it was terrifying—ski-slope steep. Rumours were already circulating that our cart was "top-heavy," but before it moved an inch, it was the envy of every kid around. As the elder, it fell to me to pilot its maiden voyage.

I gripped the rope steering and launched. The cart picked up speed—too much. Quickly, terrifyingly, I had lost control. Tony and a few others ran beside me at first, but they were soon left behind. I was alone with the beast. The end of the track—an embankment—was now rushing at me. I tried to turn, to angle along the creek bed, hoping to slow the cart down, but the weight shifted too hard. Our top-heavy Rolls Royce tipped like the Mary Rose and flung me out.

I landed hard on the upraised bolt that acted as the steering pivot. It tore a gash from behind my knee to the top of my thigh—a war wound. I screamed. Blood was everywhere. I tried not to cry, but I probably failed. A swarm of kids surrounded me—some concerned, some laughing. I never saw that billy cart again, and we never built another one. But it *looked* great—like the Leyland P76 or the Ford Edsel of billy carts: ambitious, stylish, fatally flawed.

It was around then that Tony's car sickness became a near-nightly ritual—indoors. Three or four nights a week, he'd throw up into "the green bowl," which forever reeked of vomit and Dettol. It started each night under his bed, within arm's reach. He'd roll over, throw up, then go back to sleep. Not me. I lay there in that stale, sour air. No one ever explained it. It had something to do with a "weak heart," apparently. But now, I realise it was likely migraines. No one used that word back then.

Tony was always throwing up. It was treated as part of who he was, like freckles or brown eyes. We all just lived around Tony's eternally upset stomach. I resented it—especially since an extra bedroom sat unused just one wall away.

One day, tired and annoyed, I drew a line down the middle of our shared room. "This side's mine. You stay on yours." Tony watched me, expressionless. Then a smirk spread across his face, slowly widening into a full, face-splitting grin. This wasn't the reaction I'd hoped for. He knew something I didn't. And I suddenly wasn't so sure I'd won anything at all.

We were both bitten hard by the Beatles bug. Our obsession quickly became a rivalry: who could be the *bigger* fan? The walls of our bedroom—and the wardrobe doors—soon disappeared under a collage of Beatles posters. "The Fab Four." "The Mop Tops." We hated those nicknames. We didn't love them because they were cool or famous—we loved them because the music was *everything*. Eclectic sunshine. As if they were always "sitting in an English garden waiting for the sun."

When a new Beatles single dropped, it played on the radio at midnight on the day of release. I'd lie in bed with my transistor radio under my pillow, eyes wide open, unwilling to miss the moment. Later, Tony did the same. That music became a kind of necessary element, like water or birdsong or the thrill of racing too fast downhill. For me, there was no music *but* the Beatles for a long time. The Easybeats finally forced me to widen my palette. Then Tony pulled me toward more radical, guitar-driven sounds he was starting to discover.

But before all that, we made our first public performance—as musicians.

We rehearsed "If I Fell." I took the lead vocal—easy enough—and Tony sang the counterpoint harmony, low and smooth. Our voices fit together like two streams joining a single current. We *loved* how we sounded. We were the new Everly Brothers, minus the guitars—though we improvised those, too. Two tennis rackets, with dressing-gown cords for straps.

We knew it was all a bit silly, but we were proud. We were sure our parents would be impressed.

Our bedroom sat off an entrance hall that opened via sliding glass doors onto the main living space. We set the scene carefully: sat our parents down in the lounge, facing the doors. Then, from behind the glass, I made the announcement.

"Ladies and Gentlemen, for your listening pleasure—Tony and Chris McKimm singing *If I Fell!*"

With theatrical flair, I slid open the doors. We began.

They listened—intently, almost in disbelief. We must have sounded pretty good. *We* thought we did. And when the final note ended, they were full of praise. They liked that we loved music. Our father, especially, could *feel* it, the way we did.

He always supported our musical ambitions, then and later. Years afterward, I overheard him in a conversation. One of his friends had been bragging about his kids—doctors, lawyers. The man turned to my father and asked, "And what do your boys do?"

Without missing a beat, he replied, "Both my boys are musicians."

That was good enough for me. No defensiveness. No embarrassment. He saw music as a noble calling. I loved him for that.

Around this same time, Tony and I wrote our first—and nearly last—song together. I can still see us: hunched on the edge of the bed, workshopping the melody and lyrics to *There's Someone New in Town*.

> *There's someone new in town*
> *I know. Oh yes, I do*
> *There's someone new around*
> *If I find her, I won't be blue*
> *I want her to be near*
> *To show her that I care*
> *I want to to be here*
> *So I won't be in despair*
> *Well, I've tried to be with a lot of girls before*

But they have always shown me to the door
So why can't I just kiss
The lips that I will miss
If I don't find that someone new in town

This was still before Tony had taken up the guitar. I can remember the melody of that song to this day. Years later, I finally found the chords that fit beneath it—and I still like it. Though I do wonder what possessed me to write lyrics about having "been with a lot of girls before." I was eleven. I don't even think puberty had sent in a formal notice yet.

Canberra was a clean, safe place to live—everything was laid on and laid out. It showcased both the best and worst aspects of a planned city. Too neat. Too symmetrical. Canberrans aspired to be Australia's best-read, best-educated, most intelligent citizens. There was a kind of bureaucratic unreality to the place: perpetually empty buses bearing the acronym ACTION (Australian Capital Territory Omnibus Network)—a name that felt more like satire than branding.

Sometimes it felt like someone had been hired just to follow you around and pick up any litter you might drop. (A bit like John Lennon tossing his coat, knowing someone would catch it before it hit the ground.)

There were windswept, empty plazas; vast multi-lane highways feeding into giant roundabouts; and suburbs with contradictory winding streets and houses with no front fences—because fences weren't allowed. The National

Capital Development Commission had decreed it, and everyone seemed to comply with almost religious reverence.

No fibro houses. No unpaved streets. No old cars. No visible poverty. It was a kind of antiseptic paradise. UnAustralian in its precision. And almost entirely devoid of spontaneity or soul.

This was the Canberra of the early to mid-'60s. The Canberra we left behind when our father was posted to Richmond—a Macquarie town on Sydney's outskirts where we had spent our pre-America days.

Here we go again.

CHAPTER TEN

From planned to unplanned. From polished to worn. From stately boulevards and grand architecture to narrow, uncurbed streets and fibro houses. Richmond had an air of poverty mixed with a kind of stubborn pride in the relics of yesterday. It was a small rural town, clinging to the vibrant RAAF base like a leech, with all the energy of cows stuck in the mud.

When we had lived in Canberra, the town of Queanbeyan sat just beyond its borders—messy, haphazard, a jarring contrast. Now we were living in another version of Queanbeyan. It took some adjusting.

We had become good at masking what we knew until we understood the local currency of knowledge and behavior. But I was growing tired. Reinventing myself again and again in such a short time was beginning to unravel me. I was losing track of who I was supposed to be. The only true constant in my life remained my parents and my brother. Without them, the shifting landscape of our lives would've been a screen through which the world became even more opaque.

Tony and I needed to visit the house we'd lived in the last time our father had been posted to Richmond. Seeing it again flooded us with memories: me circling the yard in my pedal car; the massive pumpkin patch in the backyard; the lane out back used by the night soil man; the carport our father had built, now rotting because he had placed the nails in the valleys of the corrugations. I remember standing on that roof as it was going up. I felt a small pang of grief for how hard he had worked.

There was the treehouse he'd built, still in the tree. The louvered windows of the enclosed back verandah, which had once channeled relief on hot days, still rattled in the breeze. And I could see Tony and me as we were—laughing, naked under the cold water of our father's hose, dancing in sheer, uncomplicated joy.

But the house was smaller than we remembered. The backyard, once an endless world of adventure, was now just a patch of earth. Even though my grandfather and I had painted it long ago, it now looked tired and unloved. We walked away from it quietly, knowing it no longer matched the version preserved in our minds.

And then there was the "Big Dipper." It had lived large in our imaginations—a thrilling drop on the road to my first school. Since those days, we had seen wonders: the Grand Canyon, Disneyland, a monorail ride beside the driver, endless highways, stormy seas, and volcanic mountains in Hawaii. But all we wanted, in that moment, was to revisit the "Big Dipper."

We arrived giddy with anticipation—and crashed into disappointment. It was nothing. A slight dip in the road. As thrilling as a puddle is to an ocean. That was the day we learned an essential truth: you can never go back. Things loom larger in a child's mind, and memory often edits for magic.

I was entering my third year of high school, and once again, assumptions were made about my academic abilities. I was placed in 3E3—respectable enough, considering the classes went down to 3E7—but I wasn't satisfied. For the first time, I advocated for myself. I went to Mr. Regan, the English master, and told him there'd been a mistake, that I deserved to be in a higher class. As I spoke, I wasn't even sure where this boldness came from. But I knew there had been an injustice, and to his credit, he believed me. He promoted me immediately.

Once there, I doubted myself as usual, thinking I was out of my depth. But the following year I was enrolled in 4E1. My brother was in the top class in his year, and now, finally, I was too. I had caught up with him—at least academically—and that meant something.

We lived in Richmond for four years—the longest we had stayed in one place. That continuity became my salvation. After initial trouble—rebelling, acting out, nearly being expelled—I was asked what was driving my behavior. I replied, "I've always been a drifter." But slowly, I settled. I appreciated having time to find genuine friends, rather than rushing into alliances with the already ostracized.

That was the dilemma in every new school: make fast friends with the outcasts who approached you first, or wait in hopeful solitude, watching the "in" crowd from the sidelines, praying someone closer to them would invite you in. In my early years, I chose the former. In later years, I learned to wait.

The best house we ever lived in was the one our parents built in Canberra. The worst was in Turner—enough to turn your stomach—but Married Quarter 209 wasn't far behind. A relic of wartime housing, it had barely been touched since Hiroshima. It was marginally cleaner, certainly smaller.

My mother faced her usual move-in trauma, but eventually, everything "came out of their boxes," and once more we were cheek-by-jowl. We'd gone from a large brick "venereal" to a fibro shoebox—an asbestos oven in summer, a fibro fridge in winter. As Tony and I grew, we took up more space, and now there was less of it to live in.

Fortunately, Richmond had what only semi-rural areas can offer: wide open spaces to escape into. Endless places to be adventurous.

Starting at yet another school meant adapting—again. In Canberra, schoolbooks were carried in haversacks slung casually over one shoulder. A Globite school case was the definition of uncool. Here, it was the reverse. After one day, I ditched the haversack for the second-largest Globite known to man. Anything to blend in.

It was absurd, really—a reminder of how arbitrary fashion and belonging can be. But we had learned one thing: when a bandwagon came rumbling by, it was best to jump on quickly—or risk being run over.

The school was a converted Second World War barracks—cold, utilitarian, and unimaginative. It marked Tony's first experience of high school, and as usual, he took it in stride. On our first day, we met up at lunchtime, as was our custom, to exchange stories about how things had gone so far. At the end of the day, we stood at our usual spot on the street outside, waiting for the bus back to the Base.

The ride took about twenty minutes each way, usually filled with chaos and the kind of noise only teenagers can generate. One afternoon, I pushed things too far. Frustrated by the bus's crawling pace, I shouted, "Careful, Mr. McKinnon, speed kills!" Even as the words left my mouth, I knew I'd crossed a line.

The bus screeched to a halt. Mr. McKinnon stood up, red-faced, and pointed directly at me.

"Get off my bus."

He had snapped—probably after years of smart-mouthed kids like me. I could feel every eye on me. Tony sank lower into his seat, desperate to avoid association with his loudmouthed brother.

I walked slowly down the aisle, trying to think how I'd get myself out of this. As I reached the front, I looked Mr. McKinnon in the eye and quietly pleaded for another chance. I promised to behave.

A long, uncomfortable silence followed before he relented: "If it happens again, you'll be walking to school."

I was only spared because Ross—his son—was my best friend. Otherwise, I think I'd have been burning shoe leather that day.

From then on, I kept quiet. I still wanted to be the bus jester, but I stifled the impulse. I'm sure Tony was relieved. He later told me that while he found the whole episode amusing, he could do without the fallout. My reputation—anti-authority, academically half-hearted—often arrived before he did. Being my brother wasn't always an advantage.

That stung. I wanted his respect. When I let him down, the loneliness cut deep. He was the best person I knew, and losing his esteem left a hollow ache I carried with me.

As time passed, Tony's talent blossomed. He became one of the finest guitarists of his generation. It remains one of life's injustices that more people didn't recognize his genius. At the time, I masked my envy in indifference. But we all knew something special was unfolding. That knowledge only deepened my paranoia. I was the plodder—someone who *might* become something with effort—while Tony was the gifted one, the artist worth nurturing.

I once asked my mother what she wanted for her children.

She said, "I just want you to be average."

It felt like the most damning thing I'd ever heard. Not to be a leader, or an achiever, or an inspiration—just to *fit in*.

It became clear early on that Tony would never simply "fit in"—and perhaps just as clear that he wouldn't be expected to. He was granted a freedom I wasn't. Where he was indulged, I met with discipline. He was allowed spontaneity; I was held to a fixed idea of what a firstborn son should be.

Still, when I reached a similar age and asked my father what he wanted for me, he simply said, "I just want you to be happy, son." At the time, I thought this was a lazy, meaningless answer. But I've come to understand how profound that wish really is. Genuine happiness is rare, fleeting, and fragile. And self-belief? That's an even taller order.

Maybe my struggle began with my birth. My mother described it as violent and traumatic. She was heavily drugged during labor, and later woke to "blood on the surgery walls" and a doctor saying, "Don't give her any more blood—she'll be dead in half an hour." At that moment, she told me, she felt relief. She began drifting into what she described as a place of peace, when she suddenly remembered she had a child to care for—alone. My father was in Korea at the time, "fighting the communist hordes." It was this realization, she said, that pulled her back. She rallied, not for herself, but for me.

I was told it took over a week before I was placed in her arms. She couldn't breastfeed—too physically depleted. I became an early formula baby. Maybe they got the formula wrong.

Doctors advised her not to have more children. She'd been told her body wasn't made for it. (Interestingly, as a child, my mother had been a contortionist. Her grandmother once warned her to stop twisting herself into knots, saying it would make childbirth difficult. Maybe she was right.)

So when Tony came along, he was a defiant second attempt—a second chance. And though he arrived frail and sickly, he met each early challenge with a kind of quiet, nineteenth-century fatalism. His fight for survival won our parents' admiration. He earned their respect through quiet strength and stoic resolve.

I, on the other hand, was more prima donna than pioneer.

At the time, our father—then CO of the newly reformed 37 Squadron—was flying C-130Es in and out of Asia. Much of his work involved transporting the dead, their remains sealed in body bags. On one of those missions, while he was away, Tony developed acute appendicitis. He got through it, I was told, by holding onto a promise: if he was brave, Dad would be proud of him. He could tell him how brave he'd been when Dad returned.

That flight back nearly didn't happen. Bad weather, low fuel, and unreliable radar made it a close call. Somehow, he and his crew made it back to Richmond. When he burst through the door, full of adrenaline and stories of daring, we listened in awe. He showed us the calculations he'd made mid-flight—scribbled like hieroglyphs all up one leg of his flying suit. It was spellbinding.

All the while, Tony was trying to tell him about the appendix. About his bravery. About how he'd waited for this moment.

But Dad was too caught up in his own story to hear it.

Finally, he gave up and, with head hanging, shuffled off to his bedroom where, no doubt, in no time, his imagination would have rescued him from disappointment. But my mother was livid. In one of the few times, I had seen her criticize my father. She told him in no uncertain terms that no matter how riveting his recent excursion into manly aeronautical adventure, his second son had undergone a crisis of some proportion and that his father had let him down. She said, "You didn't even see him. You haven't seen us since you walked into this house."

Either way, Tony would have made amends either then or soon after, but I remember the sad figure of Tony exiting his father's presence. I was also angry on Tony's behalf but didn't say anything. It was not my place.

I remember Tony being twelve when this happened. We had recently moved into the more salubrious surrounds of Married Quarter number 35015, the bottom flat of two stories. It was similar to the flat in Pearce. It was probably built at about the same time, but because it was downstairs, it was darker, moodier, and moldier than its Pearce equivalent.

Puberty hit me in the previous house. Somewhat embarrassingly, I discovered the potential of my penis in terms of giving me pleasure in the shower of this house. At the end of the bath was an electric heater that, when directed, "up" would be a shower, and "down" a tap into the bath in which one would stand to shower. One night, I must have accidentally discovered that the heat coming out of the tap was pleasurable when contacting my genitals. I soon also realized that gently increasing the heat of the water increased my pleasure until after achieving what became a very practiced balance between pleasure and pain, out of the end of my "stiffie", my by now erect penis would come, what I described to my brother as, "white stuff". Accompanied by the most incredible feeling of bodily and emotional pleasure I had ever felt.

Of course, I was having the first of many self-induced orgasms. I had achieved puberty. It had snuck up on me. Nobody warned me. Nobody told me about it save for one time in Canberra. I had come home from school, and in the kitchen at the end of the day, in my family's presence, I said I had heard several words I didn't understand the meaning of. My father asked, "And what would they be?". I replied that I thought perhaps they were rude words and that I shouldn›t use them in front of my mother. Dad said to say what I had to say. As soon as I had told cunt, and fuck, he was athletic to his feet and guiding me firmly by the elbow leading out of the kitchen and to my brother and my bedroom.

He sat me down on the bed. He sat beside me. He inquired as to whether any more words were confusing me. I said root and pull and a couple of others. He then said most of these words refer to things to do with sex. I thought, oh, here comes my birds and bees talk, but he said, "Sexual intercourse is largely like social intercourse". Immediately, he got up and walked out without a backward glance. It was as though he was running away from my reaction. He must have known how inadequate he had been, but I saw the prude in him. He was not comfortable talking about it.

So that was it. That was my talk on the mysterious world of sex. I still had no idea as to the mechanics save wondering if I spoke to the wrong girl the wrong way, I might get her pregnant. I suppose that's an alternative definition of giving head.

My hot water paradise couldn't be kept a secret. I was very keen to tell Tony all about it, although there was this lingering idea that it was perhaps a little embarrassing. I probably asked him to promise that it was our secret. I built it up so that he may have been Aladdin waiting to open the cave. I described what happened to me and said that when the "white stuff" came out, it felt so transcendently terrific to be absolutely the best feeling anybody would likely have. He seemed impressed and said that he would try at the first opportunity.

The next night, during his shower, screams of agony came out of the bathroom. We all rushed to his aid. His groin was a blistered mess, and he was in obvious pain. When asked what he was doing, he stuck to his agreement not to talk and made weak excuses about accidents, slipping, or something equally as lame and unconvincing. My parents didn't persist with the questioning, sensing that something odd was happening, and they were right after the ointment was applied. Soon after, he recovered, the burning looking worse than it was.

We spoke later, and he was angry, saying nothing had happened even though he made the water hotter and hotter, as I had indicated. We agreed that we're all different. I apologized for causing him pain. We never spoke of it again. But his testicles were not yet sperm factories, and his penis was still no more than a bladder release tube.

Mine was now a pleasure pole that would fascinate me for years. Tony soon caught up, and his sex drive became legendary and surprised even himself. He fell in love with the joys of self-abuse as his elder brother had before him. Wanking, pulling yourself, visiting Mrs. Palmer, call it what you will soon become known as "doing a Ray Brown" for Tony and me. Why? Above Tony's bedhead was a poster of the lead singer of the Whispers, an Australian band of the time, and one particularly energetic testicle evacuation saw sperm blasted into the eye of Ray Brown. We're talking two or three feet above where the same had rocketed from Tony's prone form. I didn't see it, but Tony described how concerned and surprised Ray now looked with sperm running down his cheek. We laughed. I wish I'd seen Ray before he was hastily cleaned up.

Some years later, Tony was doing a Ray, standing up, in his bedroom with his back to the door. Our mother walked in on him hunched over what she would have termed a "girlie" magazine and asked, "What are you doing?". Tony said that he hesitated briefly and then thought what the fuck? What do you do? He turned around, his hand around an erect, purple, and throbbing near orgasmic member and said, "What does it look like I'm doing"? He did not mean to be aggressive; it was just that the game was up. There was no hiding what he was doing. She, red-faced, said, "Oh, you dirty boy", and hastily exited what was, after all, a teenage boy's inner sanctum, his bedroom.

****

And he pulls them out of a hat
One by one
In awe, I say
When will they not come
You know it ain't easy
Watching him write
Songs nonstop day and night

These were the lyrics to the first song I ever wrote. There were more, long forgotten—thankfully, perhaps—but I still remember the melody. I share it not because it's particularly clever, but quite the opposite: it reflects what was happening to us at the time, living alongside Tony's emerging musical brilliance.

His talent had been creeping up on us, but suddenly, it became undeniable. Tony had an exceptional ear—possibly pitch-perfect—and an intuitive grasp of music that many trained musicians never attain. He could pick out chord progressions and replicate what he heard on the radio or television. Then he started writing songs, and it was as if a dam had broken. Dozens of songs poured out of him. To my ears, they were clever, poignant, and melodically complete. He saw them as part of a learning curve, but I saw the beginnings of something extraordinary. Some of those early ideas survived, but much was lost—sadly—into the ether. He was sharpening his craft, and in the years to come, he would write rock songs of such symphonic elegance that they could have amazed the world.

I vividly remember a sunny school holiday when Tony and his friend Geoff had set up guitars and primitive amps in our garage. They played an instrumental version of *House of the Rising Sun* to the local Base kids. Geoff and Tony were equals in spirit and skill—musical soulmates. They swapped lead and rhythm duties effortlessly. For Tony, it was a first taste of pop stardom. Within minutes, the music drew a crowd to the garage door, spilling into the backyard. There was a kind of magic in the air, like being at the Cavern Club when the Beatles were just starting out.

We knew we were witnessing something special—the ground floor of a skyscraper rise. Tony thrived in that attention. It gave him power, presence, a sense of distinction.

But great talent is a heavy burden. I would later tell him he had to learn to carry it. He would have to accept that in most musical settings, he would be the standout—the gun, the guru. Like Hawking among scientists, he absorbed what others merely sampled. Even as a boy, Tony had a gravitas that exceeded his years. And as he grew older, he became ambivalent about how easily music came to him. Not because he didn't work—he did. The guitar was practically fused to him, an extension of his body. I wouldn't have been surprised if he took it to the toilet. Like Hendrix, he and the guitar were inseparable. But with Tony, the time he put in seemed to yield more—much more—than it did for most. Certainly more than it did for his brother.

I once overheard a phone call Tony had with a mutual friend—maybe ten or fifteen years later—that perfectly captured his internal struggle. On the other end of the line was a man ready to walk away from a high-powered, well-paid job, uproot his family, and move a thousand kilometers to play music with Tony. At first, Tony was electric with enthusiasm.

"You've got to do it, mate. I love your playing. This is our shot—we've got to grab the moment. You're the only one who can help me get there."

But within thirty minutes, his tone changed. "Don't change everything just for me. Don't uproot your family. You can't leave your job—you know how badly musicians get paid."

He had swung from one emotional extreme to the other. He knew what he wanted musically—and who he trusted to help him get there—but the responsibility terrified him. Being "the man." The writer. The lead. The one others depended on. He loved the spotlight, but he feared its glare.

We were lucky to grow up with the Beatles. From 1963 to 1970, each year brought at least one new LP that seemed to define the time. In just four years, they went from "From Me to You" to "Strawberry Fields Forever." For us, the Beatles weren't just a band—they were a force of nature, a constant presence, like the seasons. Their music wasn't just influential—it infected us. Sunshine on vinyl. Bright, crystalline joy pouring out of transistor radios, car speakers, and shopping center sound systems.

They were a social phenomenon as much as a musical one. Everyone knew John, Paul, George, and Ringo. The harmony, the confidence, the playful cool—so many of us wanted to be them. Or at least *look* like them. And yet, Tony and I—thanks to our father's unrelenting rule—still looked like short-haired turds while the other boys around us started to resemble rock stars. Paul down the street could have been Roger Daltrey. Gary across the road had the look of David Crosby. But us? We were stuck in a cycle of near-scalping disguised as "modernized" crew cuts.

Haircuts came around too frequently. We both hated the ritual. And I think, in our own ways, we were scarred by it—psychologically, emotionally. If I could, I'd still have long hair. But now, thanks to hereditary baldness, I have none. When Tony died, his hair was long, down past his shoulders. I think he never stopped pushing back against that forced conformity.

I still remember, vividly, standing in front of the mirror one morning before school—about thirteen years old. I was trying to convince myself I had a fringe, comb in hand, teasing it into a curl that wouldn't stay. The cut had been too short. I tried to believe no one would notice.

But of course, they would.

Graeme would pick me up on the way to school, as usual. There was a knock on the door. Anticipating who it was, I said goodbye to Mum and opened it. Graeme burst in, doubled over with laughter, gasping, "Fuck—what have they done to you this time?"

Tony was somewhere in the house. He would have heard that outburst and instantly known the reason behind it—and the fate that awaited him the moment he stepped outside.

Another time, we begged to be allowed Amco stovepipe jeans with red stitching down the leg. You'd think we'd asked for permission to wear a tactical nuclear device. Our parents were scandalized. "That sort of American clothing" was absolutely out of the question. We were beginning to lose the will to fight, slowly coming to terms with the fact that our parents were completely out of step with the times.

Of course, what they deemed "appropriate" was so catastrophically wrong, it almost felt like a provocation. Mum revealed two pairs of loose-fitting, black, non-denim monstrosities—trousers so strange and circus-like that even a clown might hesitate. We were horrified and vowed not to wear them, but we were told we had no choice. "Nobody will notice," they said.

That was the worst lie of all.

We donned them and trudged down to the school oval for a casual weekend game. As we walked onto the field in identical humiliation, everything stopped. Balls ceased to bounce or fly. Conversations ended mid-sentence. People just *stared*. And then came the laughter—long, unrelenting, merciless.

We clung to each other, weathering the storm, longing for the Amcos with their red stitching—the jeans every other boy was wearing. We knew, even then, that if our parents had witnessed the ridicule, they still wouldn't have budged. They would've believed it was the world that was wrong, not them.

In those moments, we didn't like our parents very much. They felt impossibly out of touch.

And yet, it wasn't all so black and white. Dad, for instance, was an early believer in the Beatles—and especially John Lennon. While we still lived in Canberra, we had a tradition: a couple of mornings a week, Dad, Tony and I would drive to the swimming pool with his friend Jim and Jim's boys, Jeff and Peter, for laps before breakfast.

One morning, as we drove, Jim began his usual tirade about those "long-haired louts" who made noise instead of music. My father let him carry on for a while, and then, in a rare moment of calm conviction, he simply said, "Have you actually listened to their music? John Lennon is a particularly talented man, and their songs are quite wonderful."

We were so proud of him then. He didn't shout. He didn't argue. He just stated his truth, and for once, Jim listened. A week later, he even admitted that he'd taken Dad's advice, listened objectively, and agreed that "there was something there."

That was a rare victory.

Speaking of Tony, this might be a good time to recount the day he tried to invent a new kind of dive.

The pool had a 1-, 5-, and 10-metre board above its mirror-like morning surface. The five-meter platform was coated in smooth cement which, when wet, became absurdly slippery. Tony took his time moistening the surface—very deliberately—before announcing that he would attempt the world's first "belly dive."

He lay flat on the slick concrete, grabbed the front edge of the board, and prepared to launch himself out and down toward the water. I watched with growing anxiety—Tony wasn't exactly known for athleticism—but I had to admit: if he pulled it off, it might be surprisingly graceful.

He lay flat on the board, stomach down, and pulled with all his might. The result was not what he intended. His legs flipped up and over his back, launching into the air while his head and upper torso remained momentarily stuck—frozen in place—before finally sliding off last. He descended, horizontal, through the air, an awkward arc of limbs and bad physics. Then came the impact.

His back hit the water with a crack that echoed around the quiet pool, a sound so sudden and violent it made me wince. The bow wave he created reminded me of the *Orcades* slicing through Pacific swells. I wanted to laugh—but couldn't. It was funny, yes, but the pain on his face, both physical and emotional, stopped me cold.

Still, in typical Tony fashion, he was soon over it. We helped him to the pool's edge, where, nursing his pride, he muttered that the concept was "worth working on." He never tried it again. And though I've occasionally been tempted to test the idea myself, the memory of that descent—its graceless arc and brutal finale—has always stopped me.

****

During our time in the original, cramped Richmond married quarters, Dad spent about three months in America doing a conversion course for the Hercules C-130E. It was another example of him not caring much about where we were housed—he wasn't there. He was, as always, off serving Her Majesty somewhere far more important.

I was interested in planes, and he indulged me. He explained how the new "E" variant differed from the older C-130A models still in RAAF service. The E had larger wing tanks, positioned closer to the fuselage, and four-blade props instead of three. It was more efficient, more powerful, and— he stressed—more "sophisticated."

The day of his return was unforgettable.

We heard the plane before we saw it. Then it appeared— low on the horizon—thundering in, and Dad, letting his old fighter pilot instincts take over, buzzed the airfield before pulling a majestic wing-over and landing, as far as I could tell, flawlessly. But of course I'd think that.

After all the emotion of homecoming, Tony and I were allowed to follow Dad—alongside the Chief of the Air Staff, no less—onto the aircraft for an "inspection." Standing in the vast belly of the Hercules, we were overwhelmed by its scale, its smell of newness, and the sheer vitality of the thing. It felt alive. And in that moment, so did we.

The Chief of the Air Staff followed my father up the narrow stairs to the flight deck. Wanting to seem like more than just the pilot's kid, I remembered what Dad had told me before he left for America. Trying to sound knowledgeable, I addressed the not-inconsiderable arse of the Chief in front of me as we climbed: "Of course, the difference between the A and the E is that the E is much more sophisted."

The Chief said nothing. But from behind me, Tony, dry as a bone, said, "It's 'sophisticated,' Christoff."

Well. I was shot down, plain and simple. And he was right, of course. This was yet another example of the younger brother being just that bit sharper. There was no malice in Tony's correction—if anything, he was trying to save me from further embarrassment—but my moment of attempted brilliance had gone down in flames. My efforts at sophistication were thoroughly undercut by my inability to pronounce the word.

The next day, I returned to school. First period: woodwork— my least favorite class, ranking somewhere below a dental appointment and just above being stung by a bee. Mr. McConville, who taught the class with all the joy of a man allergic to children, was waiting as usual. That very morning, my father had landed the new Hercules at Richmond—a moment of pride splashed across the front page of the paper. I walked into the room feeling ten feet tall.

And then he said it.

"Your father can't land an aeroplane. I saw him on the news last night. He was hopeless."

Perhaps he thought he was being funny. Perhaps it was an attempt at dry humor. I didn't care. I was livid. Rigid with rage. Mr. McConville had always resented the transient nature of RAAF kids, and he'd made no secret of his disdain. But this—mocking my father's flying? This was personal. And petty.

Right then, I made a decision. "I hate this subject. I hate you. I have no intention of sitting the School Certificate exam in woodwork, and I won't be attending your classes any longer."

The only reason I was enrolled in woodwork in the first place was because my preferred elective from Canberra wasn't offered here. The only other option had been metalwork, which I abhorred even more.

His face turned beet red. He couldn't believe the RAAF brat was talking back. "You have no choice," he said. "You *have* to attend my class. You *have* to sit the exam."

"I reckon failing woodwork would be a sign that I'm actually succeeding in life," I said.

His face went from crimson to purple. I honestly thought his head might explode.

I asked how long I was legally required to sit the woodwork exam. "One hour," he said. "Right," I replied. "Then I'll sit for one hour, not even turn the paper over, and walk out."

He smirked and said I wouldn't dare—that I'd probably need the pass to go on to Fifth Form.

I said I doubted it. "If my future depends on woodwork, then the future has the wood on me."

He turned a colour I'd never seen before—something between vermilion and rage. A RAAF brat was calling his bluff.

The rest of the year played out with me in quiet rebellion. I refused to engage. And when exam day came—my first public exam—I did exactly what I said I would. I sat there for one hour without touching the paper, then stood up and walked out. The supervising teacher watched me with a gaping mouth, stunned. I wonder if I'm the only person to have never even looked at an exam.

I've always had powerful reactions to things, more inclined to oppose than to propose. Tony, on the other hand, loved woodwork. When we moved back to Canberra a year later, he took up a carpentry apprenticeship. But the cold, finger-numbing mornings and the monotony of early starts wore him down. Before long, he dropped the tools and picked up his guitar.

✸✸✸

During our time in Richmond, the Vietnam War began to dominate Australian society—especially the military. In 1969, my father, now a Group Captain, was posted to command the RAAF contingent in Vung Tau. It was the culmination of his career. While many of his generation saw World War II as the full stop on their service, Dad saw Vietnam as one last chance for action. He actively pursued the post, despite the protestations of his wife and children.

He'd already flown Spitfires in the Pacific, Meteors in Korea, and served in Borneo. But Vietnam was his final theatre. A "flyboy" to the end, he saw it as one more return to "the sharp end."

The morning he left, we stood in silence—just the two of us—locking eyes in the wind on that cold tarmac. Over my shoulder, he could see my mother, her face streaked with tears, and Tony standing withdrawn, emotionally out of reach.

I looked him dead in the eye. "What are you doing this for?"

He answered instantly, eyes flashing: "It's the sharp end, son."

That was it. Just like the brusque conversation we'd once had about sex—short, declarative, final. There was no room for discussion. He was torn, I'm sure—fear and guilt colliding—but he had always chosen the clarity of action over the fog of domesticity. He needed black and white. In war, you knew your enemies.

Within days, he would be immersed in operational life—too busy surviving to think of the family left behind.

At that point, it was obvious that Tony and I were the sons of a man who loved war, a man who found most of himself where others would retreat into themselves. I didn't find this particularly comforting, especially when I increasingly found myself on the other side of a divided Australian society.

My father was off to war for the last time, and I was off to university for the first and last time. So, the old gang was breaking up. Dad and I were leaving Mum and Tony in the flat in Richmond. My father said that I was entering the world of "radical campus philosophizing" and, in one letter from Vietnam, warned me of the dangers and wonders of the three "B's" - booze, broads and barbiturates.

I wrote this song recently; its lyrics might suggest that I was listening.

> *Marijuana, acid STP and cocaine*
> *Mescaline and opium have been in his brain*
> *But he's not demented, and he's not insane*
> *And if he had the chance, he'd*
> *probably do it all again*
> *He's eaten gold tops, yes he's taken booze*
> *Always in control, he'd never lose*
> *Always remembering the word that he heard*
> *When he was in his youth*
> *He draws the line at "ice" he doesn't need this*

He doesn't want that high or that angry bliss
It's sad, and it's stupid, and it isn't hip
He's seen people slide and slip
Into the darkest of places,
Far away from themselves
Not living a life, just living a hell
Just dancing with the devil as far as he can tell
As another life is shelved
Everything in moderation
Is what his father said
But I can't imagine that he was thinking
Of what he might put in his head.

I felt a pang of guilt returning to Canberra to continue my education, but just as my father believed he had to do what he had to do, I felt the same. There was a deeper sadness, though—an unspoken awareness that this might be the last time we all lived together under one roof. I knew I'd miss Tony, and suspected, quietly, that he'd miss me too. We never spoke of this. Ours wasn't a demonstrative family. When I left in early 1970, the mood was a strange brew of sadness, fear, and anticipation.

Years later, after a long stretch overseas with my then-girlfriend, I returned home and saw my father for the first time in over a year. In my absence, I'd picked up the hippy habit of hugging loved ones upon reunion. I greeted him with a full-bodied hug. He stood rigid, awkward, clearly embarrassed by the intimacy. I didn't dwell on it—within moments, we resumed our usual complicated handshake and that was that. Or so I thought.

A week later, without preamble, as I was packing the car to leave again, he said, "Don't ever do that again, Son." I had no idea what he meant. "Men don't hug," he clarified, still frowning. It turned out he'd been stewing over that hug for a full week. I was astonished but promised to tone it down. "Preferably not at all," he added, under his breath. It dawned on me then: in his world, only gay men hugged. That was the end of that discussion.

It was the era of long-haired men, free love, and rebellious fashion. When I returned to Richmond during university holidays, my hair was long—curling over my upside-down ears. My mother took one look and muttered, "If your father were here..." which was the adult equivalent of "Wait till your father gets home"—a phrase that once struck fear into us growing up. But I barely flinched. This new, cosmopolitan version of me was unbothered, and I could tell Tony looked at me with something like admiration. It was as though a Beatle had walked into our lounge room.

I tried to explain to Tony that the world outside the military—what many called the "real" world—was odd, gritty, chaotic, and full of contradictions, but it was where life truly happened. The military cocoon, with its hierarchy, ritual, and certainty, was comforting—but rarefied. Outside, the military was often met with suspicion, even fear. I said all this quietly, only to him. It was close to sedition in our household. Still, I planted a seed, and I saw it take root. Tony began to look forward— more than ever—to the day he could leave school and step into the weirder, wilder, more colorful world beyond.

CHAPTER ELEVEN

As if chasing ourselves around Australia, at the end of my father's posting in Vietnam, he was posted back to Canberra to sit behind a "mahogany bomber" at the Department of Air. Out of his uniform for the first time in over twenty years, he was now to spend his days at the behest of "pimply-faced public servants" who he considered ill-informed servants. He was astonished at how little and how badly they worked. He would say they worked harder at avoiding work than actually working, and you can be sure that those civilians with which he now shared his working days were equally contemptuous of him and what they would have seen as his old-world work ethic.

Having spent the last year in on-campus accommodation, it was decided that it was logical that I should return to what my father once referred to as "the blessed domestic nest." None of us knew how fraught this was. We ought to have thought about it. Still, when arrangements had been made, we discovered that "freedom boy" would have trouble readjusting to the structures of home life; I was already living said life.

I was an adult now, or so I thought, and I had mainly lived independently of my family for the previous year.

The only difference in our living arrangements in the Campbell house from last time is that I got a bedroom. No more need to draw thin white lines of embarrassment; at least I had this space to myself. But you can never go back whether you want to or not; on this occasion, I did not want to and certainly should not have.

I was fascinated at how relatively compliant Tony was and how accepting he was of what I thought to be outrageous restrictions on behavior. I couldn't understand why I couldn't come and go as I chose without explanation. I didn't know if "I would be home for dinner" or whatever. I wanted to keep living my intellectually stimulating, hyper-connected lifestyle without referencing the petty strictures of my parents' old-world values.

At this stage, Tony was in my parents' camp. He could not have known my independent life for the last year. He saw me as somewhat self-indulgent, and in that, he would have been right, but it would be fair to say that, at the least, there was a clash of wills between my parents and myself.

Tony was now in the final years of high school at Campbell High, just down the road from our place in Campbell. He didn't seem to apply himself that much to study and more to the delectable Debbie G and his guitar. Debbie was his first real love obsession, and the first time I saw her, I could understand why. She was the first of many beautiful women attracted to his stunning personality. He was a seducer through music. Women would be taken off course by his playing and his singing. Like a spider with a web made from wood and wire, he would entrap these creatures. I would look on jealously, knowing how "cool" he was, and although I was an intellectual university student, I couldn't play like him, and I didn't seem as smart as him. I was still playing with my one strum, strum and a few chords in the foothills of musical endeavor when he was on the oxygen-deprived upper slopes of the highest mountain.

Over the years, when neither of us had anything to do, we would sing together. By now, we had a few songs in our repertoire and were singing some of his songs. I can't remember them now, save for one that asked, "Taxi driver, and carry me home." Singing with him was the most elevating of things to do.

> For so long, I wanted wings
> To fly away with the things that I know
> Now that I know I have her love
> For so long, I wanted flight
> To fly away from the long, lonely night
> Now that I know I have her love

This is the chorus to one of the first songs I wrote. The bug had bitten me, and I now knew enough chords to support any early melodic ideas I might come up with. It was like finding wings. Tony's harmony in the chorus and counterpoint melody in the verse gave this song flight. I distinctly remember the feeling of being lifted, as though I was flying. Feeling weightless, our mutual efforts result in an almost visible rotating ball of energy hovering just above our heads.

I have never been able to articulate the writing process. It is of me, as it isn't for many musicians. Over the years, I have been a band writer surrounded by much better players than me, but none of them could write like I could.

I was in a band called the Reason. This was after Tony died and after a long sabbatical from music. I knew any music making would be relatively mundane compared with the music I had made with Tony. The guitarist in this band came up to me in a break in rehearsals one day, grabbed me by the shoulders, looked me straight in the eye and said, "These songs are fucking fantastic. How do you do it? I wish I could do it". In this case, I said with help from Al, another band member, that "I can't play guitar like you do, and I wish I could". This seemed to placate him somewhat, not that he had been aggressive. Quite the reverse. He was as jealous of my songwriting as I was of his guitar playing.

I was still far from being a guitarist—I still am—but I always believed that I was using the guitar as a tool to write rather than an instrument. I always made excuses for my poor playing, but early in the piece, Tony said I was not to worry that I wrote songs better than I played the guitar.

Soon enough, I was good enough to provide a rhythm bed for Tony to play over the top of. He exhibited the most wonderful musical extrapolations as long as I concentrated and stayed on the beat. Watching what would come from his imagination through his fingers was joyous. He could hear inventiveness and difference, whereas others hear the mundane and predictable. I have played with many good players, but none has shown me his capacity for fluent melody, intellectual yet organic tangential interjections, or inventions. He would conjure up moments that allowed us both to leave the room we were playing in and enter a world unfathomable and wondrous. It was like good sex in that you would come back from somewhere knowing that without each other, we would never have got to the point where we were utterly without point. It was zen-like sometimes, and it was an extraordinary privilege to have this luminous talent on hand, keen to make my songs better than they were.

> *Sitting in a room*
> *Talking "bout the likelihood of peace*
> *but you're still in the womb*
> *you won't even try to credit my pleas*
> *and I am going to show you*
> *I am going to blow the past from your mind*
> *because we've been blind for too long*
> *And aren't you tired of looking through closed eyes?*

Again, these are lyrics from one of my early songs, which featured one of his note-perfect poignant solos. We recorded this and other songs in the studio of 2xx, the ANU campus broadcast AM community radio station. I overheard Tony tell a mutual friend that this song was "as complete a song as he had heard"." Didn't I feel good?

Hearing this and other songs recorded that day and played on that station was the first time either of us had heard us coming out of a radio, and it was exciting. We could achieve a degree of detachment from the moment we recorded the songs and listened to them with some objectivity. I was able to provide Tony with this opportunity through my contacts at the university. I felt I was helping him get to where he should've been musically, and he played most beautifully, indeed, with a skill and taste way beyond his years.

While he was supposedly studying for his final year school exams and I was undertaking the second year of my degree, we always seemed to find time to play together. I find it interesting that we never really wrote together. My memory tells me that I wouldn't have presumed to have something to contribute to his songs. I thought they were so much better than mine that I may as well have been writing amoeba while he was writing elephants. A few of his songs have small contributions from me.

I recently played with two friends with whom Tony and I were in a band at one point. (The band was called Essaouira (phonetically "Essaweera" after the Moroccan town that I spent three or four months in after my university course.) It had been forty years since we had jammed, and within minutes, it was as though we had played the day before.

This time, it was a case of being able to return and be as good as remembered. You could say it had been a note-perfect reunion. At one stage, we were talking about Tony's and my songwriting. One of these friends had recorded his versions of a few of Tony's songs and a couple of mine. I am indescribably flattered that he would bother me, and I love what he has done to my songs. I told him as much, and he said he remembered my songs from forty years ago. He said he had always liked my songs and thought I wrote "better songs than your brother". He then explained that mine had an innocence that Tony's didn't. This is another way of saying I write better than I can play, and I had known that since Tony had told me all those years ago.

To be considered in the same musical breath as my brother gives me a sense of worth that is not worth describing. Suffice it to say that to be compared favorably with the best is best for me.

The following lyrics were written by my brother when he was in his early twenties. The descending melody that accompanies these words is as good as the words, and only yesterday, with the help of a mutual friend, was I able to play it for the first time. And then nothing as well as he did it over forty years ago.

> There wasn't meant to be this doubt surrounding me
> Everyone is mourning her death, and I'm on trial
> How could I have guessed
> That all the lawyers knew the rest

I was only solving my problems in a way
And I really can't see why
I was the one they were waiting for
Now I'm just a loser in this grand design of yours."
Every day seems shorter
Now I won't be waiting long
The way gods are treating me is hard and very wrong
If I knew a way, then I would bribe these honest men
But I wouldn't run away; I'd just be caught again
And I understand that I shouldn't
take life outside a war
Now I'm just a loser in this grand design of yours

He would say it was just an exercise in imagining oneself in a threatening situation; the lyrics are not literal, and they didn't know what he was talking about. It was more an attempt to create the feeling of isolation and abandonment, and at that, I think he was eminently successful. This is one of the best songs I have ever heard. It is the sort of song that should be a part of peoples' life soundtrack the way other lesser songs of that era became. As it is, there is a cell of about twenty people who know of this and other equally astonishing songs that came from the pen and mind of my brother.

At the time, he said this was not a hard song and that if I watched, I could play it "in no time". Of course, I reacted in the classic Big Brother/ Chris McKimm way and said "nah nah nah". It's too hard for me. I think that was Tony's ultimate frustration in working with me. I believe he genuinely respected my talent as a songwriter and somewhat as a singer. Still, my attitude and failure to imagine embracing positivity must have frustrated him.

There is maturity and world-wise weariness in these lyrics and the accompanying melody that lends credence to my earlier thesis that Tony was a very old soul. Barely more than a child, he writes songs of the highest sophistication. Songs of the most wonderful character almost from the moment he picked up and started picking a guitar. This supports my contention that real writers are born, not made. I can tell when a song has come to somebody, has been a gift from the cosmos, and those songs have been considered, thought about, struggled over, or, if you like, composed.

The initial idea would find Tony and me, and then if there was work involved, it was in finding words to the other verses and perhaps "finding a chorus". In later years, I have learned not to ignore the "need" to write a song. Sometimes, I must get to a guitar and get the idea out. I don't know what is happening, but it feels just like a volcano of energy rising within that often explodes into something unconsidered, innocent, and beyond thought.

Equally, like Tony, I never set out to write a song. I finish the gift that has been given to me. I don't try and drag it out of myself. I know that the products of that process are pedestrian and predictable compared to those that come to me.

****

Towards the end of the sixties, houses all over suburban Canberra had become de facto Academies of musical excellence. Hundreds of young people all over that literate city were forming bands and refining their chops in front of their friends in the living rooms of rented accommodation. Marijuana had entered mainstream alternate Canberra by now. Many a bloodstream via bongs, chillums or joints was polluted by this most perfect of musician's drugs. All of us had loved music. The excitement of music took us off course, but none of us heard music until we were stoned for the first time. The music suddenly had a vibrancy and intimacy that was impossible to describe. Like trying to explain the myriad wonders of sex to a virgin, music enveloped and engulfed the listener. Music had been black and white, and now it was color.

We consoled ourselves with the fact that the most outstanding musicians of the first half of the twentieth century, Armstrong, etc, had been "midnight tokers". We saw ourselves as part of a traditional subculture. From the beatniks came the hippies, who were called thus, initially in a derogatory sense, because the young post-beatnik generation was trying to be hip. We were alive and colorful. The "straight" society was stultifying and grey. There was always the risk of the dreaded "bust", but most of us seemed to escape the clutches of stupid drug laws. Most of the music we made, most of the time, was made while stoned. Or, as Ian Dury said some years later, it was all "sex and drugs and rock and roll", although for me, in all honesty, there was more of the latter than the former. On the other hand, my brother seemed to be getting plenty of the former and the other.

The flip side is that nearly everything you make sounds over-the-top fabulous under these weeds' influence. We would record what we had done on rough early tape recorders. Play it back the next day; it was generally not as good as we remembered. Probably, music is better listened to stoned rather than played, but that didn't stop us from going through prodigious amounts of Ganga, dope, pot, weed, grass, call it you will.

It was a constant search for the same. I remember one night, Tony had been scouting around Canberra in search of "some business" for what seemed to be our straight waiting selves, for fucking ever. Finally, headlights in the drive and a knock on the door meant that Tony had arrived with hopefully good news. On opening the door, the smile on his face indicated that he had made the connection. He produced a vial of hash oil. He sat down. I grabbed a magazine on which to roll a number. Soon, he had the "three papery" with tobacco ready to accept the oil. He proceeded to open the tube containing the same, and the lot spilled out onto his lap. As he looked at me, the expression on his face was one of devastation. I could tell he could not believe what he had done. He seemed to be saying we all know that, typically, hash oil is thicker than this. It was traditionally more like motor oil in its viscosity. This was more water than oil. It wasn't his fault, but the rest of the night suddenly looked more subdued than we had hoped.

I can't remember what happened after this. We probably rolled up whatever we could retrieve, but I remember the "little boy lost" look on his face all too clearly. He seemed so vulnerable. I felt almost maternal towards him at that moment. I would have done anything to make it all better.

The speed with which he had assembled the joint on this night was in complete contrast to his usual joint rolling technique. It could take an eternity. Without exaggeration, he could take up to twenty minutes to "Roll up" or, in the case of a bong mix, "mull up". People would be poised, anxiously seeking their chance at consciousness alteration. Tony would be holding court on something undoubtedly funny and engaging and at any other time riveting but hopelessly delaying "lighting up". This habit was probably forged in the long, cold, potentially "dopeless Canberra winter months. This is also probably why we smoke green tobacco. It was a matter of making something last longer than it had any chance of doing.

The joints coming off the talkative Tony joint rolling production line were works of art. Perfectly symmetrical tubes that it was almost an insult to suck to nothingness, but...of course, that didn't stop us, and soon Tony would be "rolling up" again, and we'd be sitting around waiting and waiting and waiting.

But playing and playing and playing. Tony and his close friends soon started to coalesce into a more formal band. Phil played drums and wrote a little. Pete played bass. One of his songs ended up in the Essaouira repertoire. Keith was a brilliant emerging guitarist and harmony singer. Tony was the principal writer and lead guitarist.

To Tony, Clapton, Page and Gallagher were the best. "Ecka" first, and then Jimmy influenced his playing. There is no shame in that. We all stand on the shoulders of the previous generation of achievers in all fields of human endeavor. The band had various names; the one I liked most was Mickey Visage. Think about it. Most people didn't, but most people do not. He had a Golden Tone valve amp that used to push out sound way beyond the bounds of thin suburban walls, and neighbors must have either loved music, wear earplugs, were deaf or were fantastically patient and indulgent because, at times, what was produced would have been as much noise, as music. Overtime skills were honed, and eventually, being paid to play was inevitable.

Somewhere along the line, I became involved in the band. I discussed this earlier. As far as I can remember, Essaouira only played two gigs. The first was an Arts College Ball. We must have been reasonable because we played our second gig at the ANU Union shortly after. We played on the same stage as Midnight Oil did later. We broke it in for them. I recently met somebody who was actually at that gig. I thought we were bad, but he said he remembered it as one of the musical nights of his life. He loved the songs, especially Tony's playing. I was pleased that he had that memory.

We would rehearse in a converted warehouse in Queanbeyan. Tony was the best player; we would've been in the cramped shed without him, but we all loved being there. We were young, and though stardom was not the ambition, the celebration of music was. We had something to say and thought we had a good way of saying it. A small, uninsulated shed on a hot summer Canberra day meant we were close. Sometimes, the atmosphere was so close that it would lead to ructions. The smallest thing would grow to monstrous proportions in that hothouse environment. I clearly remember one day we were working on a song, and one of the band members kept making the same mistake in the same spot in the same song every time. I can see Tony, patiently at first, gently suggesting to this individual that he should stop practicing the mistake. We fire up again. We get to the same point in the song, and the same person makes the same mistake. With slightly less patience, Tony would look at him and say, "Don't practice the mistake". After three or four consecutive errors, guitars would be put down, and a "session" would ensue where prodigious amounts of dope-laced air would be sucked into respective band members' lungs, and then the process would begin again. Often, when we got to that spot in that song, then the error would be erased, the correct chord played, and the day would have been worthwhile. Still, there were moments where the heat, the tension and the clash of personalities made the shed more like Dante's inferno than a place of "peace, flowers, freedom and happiness".

Tony could weave magic with a guitar. I have seen him either by design or accidentally, mostly the former, on the periphery of wherever he was. He might surreptitiously pick up a guitar, one was always nearby, and start playing—Bach to the Beatles, Sergovia to the Stones. Slowly, the room would be hypnotized by his playing. So what was a noisy rabble of people became a silent, spontaneously reverential audience.

There was no ostentation or arrogance in what Tony was doing, just transfixing playing and, at heart, a desire to share. As I have said, he could use his talent to vaguely nefarious ends, but in this situation, it was just a communication of the joy of music.

Why didn't we play again? Life intervened. By now, I was married, and my wife and I intended to leave Canberra, so our show biz ambitions ended. Years later, as another band was folding around me, standing at a urinal, mutually urinating with the guitarist in that band, I said how flat and unconcerned the band members were at their demise that night. He turned to me and said, "That's how they all end, not with a bang but with a whimper".

I thought they would go on playing without me. I didn't see myself as that important an element in the band, and although they were doing as many of my songs as they were Tony's, I had always thought they were doing so begrudgingly and that now they could get on with working on better material. I don't know why it didn't kick on. The four should have been talented and had original, fresh songwriting ideas. Tony's playing was always a feature. I loved the music they made. I was disappointed they didn't stay together, but this band's demise meant Tony was at a loose end. Ultimately, he followed my wife and me to the nineteenth-century reality of, as it was then known, the "Banana Republic." But we are getting ahead of ourselves.

The group Tony and I were a part of thought of themselves as part of the counterculture. We intended to redefine the wider society, building it on love and hope. Young and hopeful, energetic and inquiring, we fell in and out of love with each other with intensity and frequency. Lifelong friendships were formed. Hearts were broken.

We met at the university
We had the ideas of thousands before us
No more nine-to-five
We'd survey outside the system
on hope and love
But time catches all of us
And leaves us spinning 'round in circles
That seems to have no start
And just my writing this
This means that though you might think differently
You will soon depart
This is a song for you, my friend
When will we feel your warmth again
And when your journey's at an end
Come and renew the love you'll send
And as you disappear
Into sunsets
That I cannot hope to know
Will the people you meet
Come to see the love that is
Undoubtedly, yours to show

Essaouira did this song. At one point in the arrangement, we would sing the chorus acapella, which was always a challenge, especially without "fold back." However, when we got it right, our three-part harmonies were so Beatlesque that we probably should've been embarrassed. Needless to say, we weren't.

****

You could drown in drugs at this point in Canberra. Some did. Heroin was a shadow lurking behind our "straight" or moderate drug lives. Often you would get your "dope" from the local junkie who would, in turn, be financing his habit by selling dope to us. This proximity of a relatively benign, in some circumstances beneficial drug was dangerous, but for me, I saw the effect it had on the user. People became darkened and reduced, mumbling often incoherent versions of their former selves. I couldn't see the point and never tried it. I tried just about everything else but not smack. In my observation, the most intelligent and the most stupid people I had met became junkies. People in the middle, the ruck, the scrum of humanity, were rarely seduced.

Tony fell in love with the most beautiful of young women. Patricia was a doll-like, perfectly proportioned, post-pubescent picture of pulchritude. She was damaged and had been variously used in her life. She hovered on the edge of Tony's inner circle of friends and ingratiated herself through her sexual willingness. I think she was abused as a child and had a very fragile self-belief. She ended up being a full-blown heroin victim. Many of Tony's nights were spent sitting up, holding her tongue out of the back of her throat, so completely comatose was she. Often, just this side of overdose, she would not have survived without Tony's literal and figurative support.

Herein lies a complicating factor and something that Tony never got over. In 1974, my father was posted to the Royal College of Defense Studies in Belgravia in London. Tony was encouraged to accompany them, as this was the chance of a lifetime. His gratis opportunity to see more of the world. To do this, Tony would have to leave Patricia. By now, an item, they were as in love as those new to love can be, but it was simply heart-wrenching for Tony to leave her. He knew she had a very tenuous grip on life. He was worried that she might come to harm if he left her.

Against his best wishes, he went with his parents to a flat on Wimbledon Park Road, just up from the famous strawberry and cream center of tennis. He couldn't and didn't try to forget her. At one stage in their sojourn, there was no doubt Dad was off either fighting the communists or learning how better to fight them. He and our mother spent a week in France. Whilst there, Tony cogitated on Patricia. He missed her terribly and worried about her constantly, convinced that he had let her down. He wrote this about her and his not being with her when it was all he wanted, and she did, too.

> *I've got a cold room on the via Firenze*
> *And I guess if I loved you, this is the end*
> *I think I'm going crazy, but that isn't new*
> *I get so tired I get lazy as I get over you*
> *And it's true I'll do all that I can*

Because it's true, you make me feel like a man
I stand in the plaza
I hide in the crowd
My laughter is lonely
And my jacket too loud

And then reflecting on the journey that had brought him to Europe this holiday with his money and away from her

It's a short step from the cabin to the handrail
It's a single stride. Forget your pride. This is blackmail

Unfortunately, the worst happened. Soon after he left her in Canberra, Patricia was dead—a too-beautiful being brought to a too-ugly, too-early demise. Tony blamed himself. He emotionally flagellated. He knew this was going to happen. If he had been there for her, she would still be. He was very angry with himself and his parents. I don't think he ever forgave them for pressuring him to go to England with them.

Like any red-blooded male, he enjoyed her sexual favors, but I think that, at heart, he loved and appreciated her. We had grown up under the influence of a man who genuinely loved and respected women. As carnal as the next man, he understood that a person's sexuality was the least important aspect of self. He saw women as people, as John Lennon said, "the better half of the sky".

Just before Tony smoked a bong one day, the person he was with sprinkled some white powder onto the top of the tobacco/dope mix in the cone. He hesitated but proceeded to light the bong and then inhaled. The rush started with a tingling in his feet, then pulsed up his legs, torso, and neck, where this intense energy exploded through the top of his head. He said he had never felt so very, very good. He felt wonderful. He knew something was wrong. Even the best heads wouldn't elicit this euphoria. It was soon established that the white powder was heroin.

One week later, despite his experiences with his girlfriend, he watched himself bring a needle towards his expert girlfriend-assisted, raised vein. He froze, scared by what he was about to do. He wondered how quickly he had come to see what he was about to do as a norm. He had only smoked it up to this point. As far as I understand it, he has never gone near it again.

Alcohol was a problem drug for Tony, he took to it and it took to him. Not a big man, he tried to keep up with his often larger contemporaries in its consumption. Perhaps, like his father, he didn't know when to stop, and many nights would be reduced to mumbling incoherence or absurd acts of daring. (I have heard stories of his climbing the top of shop awnings in Queanbeyan in the early hours of an inebriated night. Of his driving back into Coffs Harbor on the wrong side of the road, oblivious to trucks and cars that had to swerve to miss him. He was famous for his propensity to "Noah's ark" - bark - vomit). One of his girlfriends speaks of his hanging precariously out of the car she was driving while they were speeding down the highway). The same woman said that Tony should never have touched that drug. That turned him into a monster. Not violent, as I understand it, but somebody in that state prone to idiot excesses that, the morning after, would be remembered, if remembered, with embarrassment and remorse.

One night, towards the end of my University days, my father was having a party, an obligation of his status in the cocktail circuit of Canberra. My father was one of those people who could do without people. A person who rarely sought out another person, when he was forced to be a raconteur, an entertainer, he was brilliant at it. Ironically, my parent's parties were famous for the garrulous host, my father. Ironically, I have seen him closing the door on people who had come to seek his counsel and, in that instant, say something like, "Loser, why does he darken my door"?. But while inside my father›s house, this individual had thought himself close to and essential to my father.

So, as one of Dad's guests exited the party in the early morning hours, he returned to tell my father that somebody slumped under his car in the garage. My father went to investigate to find Tony, virtually comatose, where he had been placed by his "caring" friends. By now, I was aware of the ructions, having exited my room to see my father propping Tony up, Weekend at Bernie's like, introducing him to his remaining party guests. "This is my son," he said whilst this dissembling, disheveled mess dribbled beside him.

Another time, whilst visiting my parents at their newly built, nearly bankrupting home at Banora Point, he had gone into

Coolangatta to watch a band. He consumed too much alcohol and proceeded to drive himself home. The next morning, my parent's house was son bereft. Dad went out looking for him. He found him in his car precariously balanced on the edge of the highway near the entrance to the Boyd Bay bridge. He must have stopped there because he hit something. Otherwise, Tony and his car would have gone swimming.

****

It is 1974. I am driving my first car, a 1967 white 1100cc Corolla, the second model released in Australia. (This car was known to my university friends and me as "Super C". This car made me cool. I was the only one in my circle of friends who owned a car. I was popular. (Pathetic, isn't it). Tony is sitting beside me. We are going to the university where my final year Arts degree results are "on the noticeboard". We're not particularly talkative. This is most unusual for Tony. He seems slightly pensive. I can't focus on why, but he is not his usual voluble self.

We park the car and go to where the results are pinned up. I am somewhat apprehensive. I have used my fourth year at ANU to escape the clutches of the crushingly conservative, formaldehyde world of the law, with its crusty dusty tedium and with seven passed law units credited as three arts units; if I pass these units, I am a Bachelor of Arts (pass, just as I expected). There is a crush of variously, crushed, expectant, elated or, more generally, simply accepting people. I elbow my way to the front. I found my name, and to my astonishment, I have passed one unit and achieved a credit pass in the other two. I am absurdly happy. Outrageously happy. I felt like dancing a jig. Until this point in my particularly stellar academic career, I had done no more than pass. That was my motto. Do enough to pass—live life.

I pushed back through the crowd and found Tony waiting for me. I told him the good news and how surprised and happy I was at getting two credits. (My body language and face-splitting smile probably suggested as much). This reflected that I had enjoyed my last year at uni. Tony remained unusually silent. As we were walking back to the car, he asked me, "Does this mean that you have a degree? That you are a Bachelor of Arts"? I replied in the affirmative. He gave me a strange look. It seemed to say that he thought there was something out of balance. Somehow askew.

He congratulated me. He was genuinely happy for me and proud as only one sibling can be of another. There was not a hint of jealousy or the suggestion that I didn't deserve or hadn't earned my degree. He said nothing more, but I think he might have been reflecting that in the time I had been working, if that is not too strong a word, toward my degree, he had done the final year of school twice and not done at all well on either occasion.

He would have protested that the first time was not his fault. He said he and his mates had made a pact that they wouldn't do anything in each exam. Tony didn't. They did. They passed.

Tony didn't. The second year failed to achieve because he had lost interest by then. Guitar and girls had taken over his life by then, and he said he couldn't care less about his school results.

That is true, but I would also contend that this is one of the few times in our life together where I had done something that he hadn't. I think he was as surprised as I was that I had pulled it off.

But he was happy in his status as one of Canberra's emerging guitarists. At one stage, I introduced Tony to the man who had shown me my first chords, and they 'jammed'. I had raved to Bernie about Tony being as good as he was. There were not many better than Bernie; before coming to study at ANU, he had been a part of the burgeoning Melbourne music scene. He knew what he was doing; he knew his chops. After the jam, my friend said that my brother had something and would probably be successful in music.

Around this time, Tony auditioned for a band. Aspirants were to meet this day at an advertised venue. Alan, a man who was to become an essential figure in Tony's life, had brought himself from Cootamundra to so audition. Like Tony, he had been playing for years, and he was an outstanding guitarist in his own right. He had intended to audition as the lead guitarist of this fledgling band. Not an arrogant man, he was nevertheless knowledgeable. He possessed a chutzpah that saw him walking confidently into threatening environments without a facial twitch to reveal the suggestion of inner turmoil. He would have made a perfect lead guitarist for this potential band.

He watched this small man, Tony, walk up on stage to join the rhythm section. He plugged in his guitar and started to play. Within minutes, Alan knew he had seen somebody play as if he could only imagine being able to play. Immediately, he decided he would audition as the band's bass player. As I understand, he had never really played the instrument before, but it would seem that they struck up a musical partnership based on mutual musical respect. Tony thought Alan was as good a bass player as he had worked with, and Alan knew he had found the best guitarists.

****

Nobody can be good at everything, and Tony was, initially, not good at riding motorbikes, but as was always the case with something that he desired that was just out of reach, if he wanted to ride, he would. This entailed me spending, according to my mother, "an inordinate amount of time" helping him learn. I didn't mind helping because he was my brother and because this was something I could do, but he couldn't. He took a long time coordinating his right-hand throttle with his left-hand-controlled clutch. No amount of tutoring would see him do anything other than stutter clumsily, vaguely in the direction he intended the machine to go.

He would look at me with an expression that said, "This shouldn't be that hard. YOU can do it after all". After another failed attempt at forward propulsion, he would dejectedly get off the bike, and I would show him again. Each time, he would be convinced that he had got "it", but each time, he hadn't. He was almost in tears sometimes. This went on for some days. Every day after school, I would see Tony and I on the road at the front of the Campbell house, alternatively getting off and on. I was even reduced to running beside him, my hand over his left hand, trying to give him the "feel". I kept telling him that it would 'click", and he would be away when it did.

It did, and he was, and I rarely saw the motorbike again.

It and Tony went off to join his "bush-bashing" mates. They all had better, more powerful off-road bikes, so Tony's motorbike was unsuitable. It was a street bike designed to transport a university student conservatively to his early morning lectures, and very quickly, it became bashed by the bush rather than the reverse, but in the process, he became a perfect rider. He could ride with flair and proficiency when he progressed to bigger and better. I like to think that my patient tutoring in the two-wheeled art had something to do with this.

There was an incongruity in how Tony and his poetic, musical mates met the bush. Off-road bikes in those days were particularly loud. Still, the fashion was removing the baffles from the muffler to make them even look at me loud so that such machines ridden through closed suburbia would resonate with a violent echo that could be heard from blocks away. Tony said that one day they had been going blat blat blat through the bush, making the usual cacophony of environment-threatening noise when they all pulled up together, switched off their motorbikes and from their elevated position looked back down a deep green conifer-clad valley, and they all looked at each other and "felt the serenity". They mutually agreed just how beautiful and peaceful it was and then fired up and went blat blat blat back to the city that fringed this magnificent made-for-trail bike riding forest.

CHAPTER TWELVE

In their hundreds, Egg cartons had followed me and whoever I was living with for many years. Tony and I had thought we would use them when, one day, we built our recording studio. They act as magnificent soundproofing. We had been addicted to recording music since our father returned a Sony "Sound on Sound" tape recorder from one of his Asian adventures. Dad gave the machine to the two vibrating boys, anticipating that they would tell us about the wonders of Sound on Sound as he did so. He told us that we could record onto one track and then return to the start and play over that track onto the second track. Revolutionary.

Whilst still in Canberra, we had done some studio recording, and one of the reasons we were reasonably efficient in the studio for the first time was the hours of practice we had had on the Sony at home. We had got over "red light" fever. We were practiced in turning it on when we had to. Twice, Essaouira went to Glo Audio recording studios. The first time we set up live, we recorded the band with inadequate baffles or sound walls between us to give some microphone separation. We didn't play our best because we couldn't see each other. But the band did as well as it could in the circumstances, and given the band's relative inexperience in this environment, we thought we came away with something that was representative of what we could do. It was not as polished as we would have liked, but time and money precluded anything more sophisticated.

At a party some years later, I heard the producer say to a fellow party guest that our band had been the best that had been in their studio. All I can say is that there must have been some pretty average music recorded in that converted garage studio. With all due respect, it was more of a garbage studio.

The second time, we recorded two songs with a view to one being a single. I had become a victim of the radical campus philosophizing that my father had warned me about because I wrote this song with Malcolm Fraser and his imperial ambitions in mind. I must have written at about the time of the dismissal. Tony had also drifted to the "left" by this time and had become quite righteous in embracing the counterculture ethic. So he took to this song with a gusto. He added a guitar bridge, as a middle eight, that lifted it to another level, and therefore, Going Right is as close to a true collaboration as we had written up to that point. What Tony did to it made it a better song, but he would acknowledge that his contribution would not have had a leg to stand on without what I had brought to the table.

So all this talking on the telephone
Won't make it easy or a better home
It just leaves us hanging on this lonely wire
And then he tell us of Election Day
Four out of five. well, this is hardly the way
To run this country at the whim of you side
I think I'm leaving
I'm sick of lies
It's always going right
Always going right
Leaving those who are left
And when its gone wrong
And when its gone wrong
Where on earth will they be
They'll be outside
All that lost energy

Keith played the drums as we recorded this song. The second guitarist in the band was dragged into playing the drums on this track, and he did a sterling job. We used the first take. He complained that he was "just getting into it", but it was decided, much to his chagrin, that what we had was what we needed. He was frustrated, if not angry, that he was not allowed the chance to do the drumming properly. We thought he had. I haven't heard the song in years, and I am sure the drumming stands up.

As with most things I have been involved in over the years, it all came to nothing. I intended to move to the north coast of New South Wales to support my then-wife in her legal practice ambitions. I was to practice anonymity. Leaving Canberra was an easy thing to do. Cathy and I didn't want to be "Canberra" people. We wanted a life full of Queanbeyan. Our destination was the hinterland alternative community of Bellingen. I don't know what we intended, but we were part of the educated baby boom, leaving the city diaspora in search of a life more organic, more natural, less industrial and more communal. We found some of this and lost each other in the process.

We had been living on the coast for about a year when Tony said that he had decided to move out of Canberra and thought where I was would be the best of places. I didn't argue with him. Although in our latter years in Canberra, apart from when we would mutually sweat over the band in rehearsal or performance, we led essentially separate lives. Tony had his group of friends, and I had mine. Now, however, I was his advance party, his scout, and I was the one with some knowledge of how to survive out of the bureaucratic comforts of the national capital. I was so excited at the prospect of our making music; my first thought was the egg cartons.

So, as he is readying himself for his departure to Coffs Harbor, I am building a frame inside a spare room in the house that Cathy and I were renting that I could see us turning into a recording studio. I was now the proud owner of a TEAC 3440 reel-to-reel tape recorder. This was sound on sound on steroids. With this machine, one could drop down, consolidating tracks as one did so, to an extent whereby we could record up to, from memory, eight tracks. All pre-digital, there was a loss of signal and an increase in "white" noise or "hiss" each time tracks were thus consolidated, but we would hear past that and to what we wanted to hear.

In the meantime, I had managed to acquire fridge-size cardboard boxes, which I thought we could then attach to that frame and then somehow attach the nomadic egg cartons. I hadn't thought exactly how that attachment would occur, but I knew it would be sorted at one point.

Duly, Tony arrived, and old Holden (The Mongrel) overlapped with old wares and memories. First, I showed him the frame I had built and what I intended to do with the cardboard. He saw this as a valid option. I think he was quietly impressed by my inventiveness. It was just so organic that we would be re-recording music. It was as logical as the air we were now mutually breathing. It was as important as that as well.

Both Cathy and I were working. Tony was to stay with us "until he found his feet". The first day I went to work, after his arrival, I came home to the "studio" completed. During the day, he individually attached each egg carton, top and bottom, and on each side, with individually formed wire hooks. It must have taken him the entire day. He must not have done anything else. I thought what he had done was magnificent, and between us, we had come up with a soundproofed cell in which we could record, forever, in our time and without having to pay anybody for the privilege. He had even fashioned a door out of one of the fridge cartons.

It was unbelievably sophisticated, given the nature and materials in its construction. And the sound. It was fantastic. The best acoustics of any room or space I have recorded in. All the tops were taken off the vocals. There was no "splash". It was studio-quality sound. We were proud of ourselves and looked forward with childlike anticipation to the music we would make in what was essentially a big cardboard box.

The only problem was that the studio was akin to being in a high-end Swedish sauna as the summer approached. We basted ourselves in that space. We would look at each other, me through humidity-fogged glasses and see each other streaking sweat, but still, we would persist. We recorded many songs this way, and we probably lost much weight. Needless to say, we were in paradise. There was nothing better in the world to do. We were doing it together and without reference to anybody else. For as long as we were in this cardboard cocoon, there was nobody and nothing else in the world. It was our world. It was the best world. It was a "magnetic madness".

At the end of his life, there were taped songs from ten to fifteen years in spools ranging from four to ten inches. No doubt those tapes would have oxidized by now, and the memories mangled by passing the time, but I would love to hear them today. I have to say that in my life of music, whenever I record something, it is immediately unsatisfying. There is always the thought, "Is that all there is"? Nothing is ever as good as imagined or conceived; over time, I have learnt that there is never anything definitive. What you have is a record of the best of yourself, then.

Equally, when I find something from the past, I am invariably of the opinion that it is better than I remember it being, so I would imagine there are some gems lost to chemical reaction and physical decay. I will never hear them again. Nobody will, but I have memories of intimate, inspiring times shared. This is unique to Tony and me.

Others had musical moments with my brother. When he died, at the wake afterwards, several people spoke to me of how inspiring he had been to them personally, particularly on a musical level. But he was my brother. There was a chemical. Biological and psychological empathy, emotionally and physically, that nobody else had with him.

After all, he had followed me to the North Coast.

> *Today is today*
> *Tomorrow will be just the same*
> *Who's to blame*
> *For a life that's so mundane*
> *I feel my hair is crawling*
> *I hear my brother calling*
> *DREAM*
> *Wishing till insane*
> *That I could live with you again*
> *So much to say*
> *I'm not surprised you tried to run*
> *Lonely one*
> *Life can be so hectic*
> *I used to take it out on you.*

I read this as a song to and about me. Others say it is referencing Patricia. I think "my brother calling" is a bit of a giveaway. Anyway, I choose to hear it that way. I don't care if I am wrong; it suggests a need to be with me and respect what we had musically and personally. I read it as him telling me that what we did together, musical and otherwise, was as important to him as they were to me. In turn, this is important to me and gives me an insight into why he musically put me ahead of others. I was his muse as much as he was mine.

This is one of Tony's songs Keith recorded after Tony died, and his versions are profound in their beauty and respect for Tony. He was as enamored of Tony as I was. They had a special musical bond that predated Essaouira. They had played in a duo together and had shared many musical intimacies that only Keith could know about. Keith is the only person alive who can play and interpret Tony's music. We all owe him a massive debt because this memoir would not have happened without him sending me his spin on those songs.

At one stage, when Tony was working as a chain man at the Canberra Department of Works on his first day, he was asked by his fellow workers what his name was. His response was, "Hank". Because he knew himself to be as "unhank" as could be imagined amongst those who met him there, he was Hank as much as he was Tony. Keith's first son is called Hank, and this is an homage to Tony. It's fair to say that Keith misses Tony as much as I do. He would say it was unfair that life took

Tony away. He would say that he loved him like a brother. I know how he feels.

****

Tony lived with us for a while, and then he met and fell in love with the beautiful, intelligent, sharp-witted, word-playing Linda.

I could travel 'round the world
I'd never find a prettier girl
We're so lucky boys
We're so lucky to be
Born into this world
That manufactured this guitar
Now, if you're feeling low
Close your eyes and listen to me
Coz I'm the blues healer
Trying to take your pain away
Looking for a sunny day
So if those blues you are feeling
Put them on a passing train
And learn to love yourself again

Linda was not only as beautiful as all the other women who had been attracted to my brother, but she was also his intellectual equivalent. I used to sit and watch them bounce off each other. Sharp word play and nuanced tangential humor that would leave me slack-jawed in disbelief. It was a joy to watch them in full flight. They were a fantastic match for each other, and in the early years of their relationship, they were physically and emotionally beautiful together. They were a model couple. They loved each other.

However, just before he died, they had come apart. In the end, more open wound than open heart, I can see Linda physically looming over the top of a, in a corner, on the floor hunched, the shell of my brother her forcefully telling him that she had "had enough. I'm sick of your bludging. You never pay the rent. I am over it". I can see him looking up at her and pleading that he had nowhere else to go.

This is close to the last memory I have of my brother, and it is not a pretty one. This is not meant in any way as a criticism of Linda. Quite the reverse; I can understand why she came to that conclusion.

Some time previously, Tony had a massive abscess from a rotten tooth. One side of his face expanded to fill the room he was occupying. I asked him why he wasn't doing anything when I saw it. He must be in pain, and if he didn't do something soon, his system may well be poisoned. He mumbled through a distorted visage that he couldn't afford to do anything about it. I was angry with him. I said I would pay for whatever it would cost him to have his face return to a standard dimension. He was thankful, and the situation was remedied over the next few days.

That night, I remember saying to my new young wife, Alana, that I would have to accept that I would be propping up

Tony financially for the rest of my life. Therefore, I related to Linda's frustrations. She had and still does love him enormously. She said this was the best man she had known or would know for her.

However, I can remember there was a family member we knew as Uncle Will. He was my father's brother, and he was an artistic drifter who would spontaneously inject himself randomly into the lives of his extended family. Then, just as quickly, they disappear again. He was known to be clever and original of mind. He was also known as "a charming waster". In many ways, Tony was the Will of his generation.

Towards the end of his life, his final original band, Loup Garou, had collapsed around him, and he was playing in a covers band. He had been headhunted, and it was accepted that he was the best guitarist in Coffs, but Tony's heart wasn't in it. I think this was part of the cause of his in-front-of-a-mirror exit from life. I think he was at a pivotal point in his life when the real world of adulthood loomed, and it frightened him. Suddenly, he was treading water where he had been swimming upstream with vigor and purpose. And so he lost the Will to live. As discussed, as a young person, he was not well. But he had a lust for life that probably only his father could understand. They both loved being alive as long as they had a purpose.

My father didn't last long after he was no longer allowed to fly, and the same thing, I think, happened to my brother. As long as he believed he had a future that he could project positively into, he could override his physical limitations. Still, as soon as believing became an effort, he failed to find the energy to maintain his life. I think he saw a dark future. I think he sought the light.

****

Penny Lane, Strawberry Fields,
Places real and unreal
As real as my memory allows
And if I had my way
I'd live back there today
And laugh at me as I am now

When Tony was alive, we sang this song a lot. It was one of his favorite Chris McKimm songs. He played this staggering guitar figure solo that lifted the song above us. I loved that he loved my songs. I was in awe of his.

After he died, I recorded this song with Pete, Linda's hugely musically talented, inventive, and thoughtful son. Pete had been influenced by Tony's playing and, like me, could not have had a better tutor. In some ways, working with Pete was completing a cosmic circle. Of all the guitarists I have listened to and played with since Tony died, Pete is the one who comes closest to Tony in style and original ideas. He can play almost any guitar genre and plays with a melodic fluency that only my brother could best. I can't think of a greater compliment to pay Pete.

I wrote another verse to the song after he died.

I remember him now
With his head in the clouds
Refusing to ever come down
Now he'll be forever young
Never under time's gun
With a face still unlined and so proud

He and I played a gig at a local bowling club. It had been hard work. Though not overtly hostile, it was obvious that the audience wanted more of what they knew and less of what was new. Tony held it all together, of course. He was like a scaffold, a rock, a smiling, positive, encouraging support and without him, I could not have stood in front of people. He made me feel as though I had a right to be there. At the end of the gig, we drove our laughing way home, looking forward to a post-gig "sesh". When we got to his house, empty of his girlfriend for reasons I can't remember, he produced about half a deal of THC-packed heads. We started into the bag. Within an hour, the bag was nearly empty. I sit cross-legged on the floor before the mull bowl, handing Tony another bong. By now, he is looking at me with the reddened, hooded eyes of somebody well and truly blitzed. He takes it from me, and almost with an air of "Oh must I" resignation, he proceeds to light and pull. Smoke in an absurdly large, room-fogging cloud leaves his lungs. He hastily hands the bong back to me and then gently falls backward so that he is now flat on his back. He bursts into what our mother would have called "a fit of the giggles". I fall back similarly. We are now looking at each other, our faces inches apart. He says, barely coherently, "That's it, I've done it. I'm a G.I., a gibbering idiot."

I laughed so hard I nearly wet myself. Sometimes, laughing is almost orgasmic in its liberating intensity. I think that's why I love it so much, and much of the reason that I loved my brother so much was that so much of the time, he was making me laugh.

****

Before Tony moved to Coffs Harbor, Mick Lee and I had formed a trio. Lee was on congas, Mick was on mandolin and bass, and I played guitar. This was the first time I had played guitar in front of an audience, and it was daunting, to say the least. I have never liked the sound I made with a guitar, and now it was amplified, filling up the beer garden of the Park Beach Hotel Motel. Or, as the locals would say, the "Hoey Moey". We mostly played with drunk surfers who I noticed were already some years younger than me. This is when the Sandman ruled. The purpose-designed "shaggin" Wagon" or "fuck Truck" was ubiquitous in the adjacent car park.

> *Unemployed surfers*
> *Come here from afar*
> *You know that they'd rather*
> *Live out dull days in the sun of Coffs Harbor*
> *They smoke marijuana*

That's grown in bananas
You know that they'd rather
Live out dole days in the sun of Coffs Harbour
See them breasting the bar
On Sunday afternoon in Coffs Harbour
Drunken gals with their guys
With wild acid eyes in Coffs Harbour
Unemployed surfers
Drive 'round in vans man
Combi's and Bedford's,
Holdens and Falcons
Lined up on the Sandman
Unemployed surfer
Live on the beaches
Make love on the beaches and stay out of reach
As unemployed surfers
See them down at the Hoey
On any afternoon in Coffs Harbour
Drunken gals with their guys
Where the waves meet the sky in Coffs Harbour
If the connection you miss
Spend your dole getting pissed in Coffs Harbour

I had always raved about Tony's playing so that when he arrived in Coffs, he attended a rehearsal of Rocksoft (I always hated the name). It was quickly apparent that we were better with Tony, and they readily agreed to his joining us. The residency at the Hoey most Sunday afternoons meant that we soon had the beginnings of a following. This was a first for me, and I enjoyed the feeling, given that much of our repertoire was the songs I wrote at the time. Tony's songs were soon a part of what we were doing. One Sunday, there was a table of Indigenous Australians enjoying the music they heard that sunny afternoon. They were loud and vociferous in their approval. Tony suggested we do one of his songs that we had been rehearsing.

> We kill the blacks
> Cause they couldn't read the bible
> We stole the land
> Lord Bathurst wrote the title
> We kill the rivers
> We kill the forests
> We lose our soil to the
> We dug up the gold and put a white
> man's price on this land
> We deny the fact
> so vain we build upon it
> The Immigration Act
> White Australia is so ironic
> We all dream about owning our
> own piece of land someday
> But beads and mirrors, now, who do we pay
> For this land
> This land does not belong to you and me
> This land belongs to the Aborigines.

It was the last song of the set. We put our instruments down and melted into the crowd. Tony walked past the Koorie table and one of them said something like, "good song brother but we just come 'ere to get pissed". Somewhat deflated, Tony walked towards the bar and a waiting beer. He spoke of it later. I said I saw it as a case of ideology crashing into reality. He agreed but was nevertheless disappointed that the very group of people for whom he was trying to be a white middle class, aware spokesman, weren't really interested in his politics.

Another "whimper" later and Rocksoft has gone limp and we are once more between bands. I am now divorced and living in a small house nestled in bananas in the folds of hills above the coast. Mick from Rocksoft , Tony and I set ourselves up to do some home recording in the living room (to give it a grand name way beyond its shed like reality). We called ourselves, The Bronchial Bay Boys. I thought this was an obvious but reasonable punning allusion to the reality of living in Coffs (cough cough) but surprisingly over the years I have had to explain it more than it has been understood. When I do explain it, people inevitably say something like, "fuck, that's clever. I would never have thought of the connection". Not so funny punning then.

We had all the instruments we needed except for drums. Tony had a bass kick peddle. He attached this to a large cardboard box, which was our kick drum. He fashioned wire into a circular configuration that, when struck, resembled either a ride cymbal or a hi-hat. I simply don't remember what he used as a snare, but with this kit, we recorded over a dozen songs. This was before the days of drop-in, so everything had to be recorded live to tape.

It was easy enough with experienced musicians like Mick and Tony, but Tony's drum kit was still ridiculously primitive, and only the most talented people could have produced anything resembling a real drum sound. He did, and he did this while chasing the kit around the room, as, unanchored, the whole thing would subtly slide away from him.

We both loved where we were now living. I wrote this song for the beautiful woman who would become my second wife and the mother of our two lovely daughters. Alana was the most beautiful woman I had ever seen; falling in love with her was the primary reason I fell in love with this part of the coast. Again, the fact that I was making music with my brother meant that life was as good as it had ever been. I had the love of my brother, my soon-to-be wife and the most astonishing geography as a backdrop to sun-filled days of happiness and contentment.

> *The view is spectacular*
> *I can see for miles*
> *And though I may have seen the back of you*
> *I still see your smile*
> *Reflected in Split Solitary*
> *here where the bananas grow*
> *I will make my home*
> *There is no place that I would rather go*
> *To call my own*
> *I've been gazing on Split Solitary*
> *You make me feel so comfortable*
> *There is your smile*

You make me feel "unruffable"
And given my past, that's wild
I'd been living in split solitary
I had been
Living in split solitary

★★★

Loup Garou was Tony's last original band. It was initially made up of myself, Tony, Mick, Phil (from Canberra and Essaouira) and Dave, also an ex-pat Canberran. After some time, Mick dropped out and was replaced by Alan, yet another refugee from the national "crappytol". We rehearsed in a large house that two band members rented. The house was a reasonably modern dwelling atop a large hill that afforded panoramic views of the beautiful hinterland and coast below. It was an inspiring place to work and write. During this period, Tony wrote a collection of the most amazingly sophisticated, thoughtful, profound, enigmatic, funny, riff-heavy ballads to heavy metal rock songs. It was an outpouring that saw the synthesis of years of absorbing the best that all forms of music had to offer. It was astounding the quantity and quality. I could not have been more proud and more in awe and all the more with the feeling that I didn't belong.

I was not a good enough guitarist to play in this band. Dave was a perfect lead and rhythm guitarist. Even Phil, the drummer, was a better guitarist than me, as was Alan, the bass player. So, one more time, I was reduced to being the singer because I couldn't be anything else. I didn't think of singers as musicians then and felt embarrassed and out of my depth. Tony was his usual reasoned and patient encouraging self, but there were times when I just couldn't do what he and the rest of the band wanted me to do. Therefore, the day came when I said I wanted out. The band members protested ritually; perhaps their heart was in it, but I didn't feel it. I felt confirmed in my decision.

Tony and I had to drive home with Mick at the end of the day. Tony and I had a ride-long bickering session, the likes of which probably only brothers can have. I could see it was boring, Mick, but we continued. Nothing was ever resolved. It was one of those pointless, caustic, circumlocutory conversations that rise in volume and anger. Tony was in the front seat beside Mick, who was driving. I was talking and alternatively shouting at the back of his head. He kept insisting that I should be more confident. That I was more talented than I thought I was. That I wrote better songs than I thought I did. That he wanted me in the band, and why else had he moved to the North Coast if not to play music with me? I wouldn't hear. Finally, in exasperation, he swung round, looked me straight in the eyes and said something very close to "that'd be right. You fucking hate life, and I fucking love it. I bet I'm gone long before you are, and that pisses me off."

We weren't to know how soon he would be so right. All this did was remind me of a time when I had failed my second-year high school exams, and my father had given me what he would call a "bollocking" because I hadn't achieved a level he thought I could or should. The dressing down had been more appropriate to somebody who had set fire to a city block lacked a city water supply with poison, or had planted a nuclear bomb under the Department of Defense, not somebody who had failed a mid-year test exam.

I was probably in shock, but Tony and I went for a late evening bike ride, me dinking him around our neighborhood. During the ride, I said, "I reckon you and Dad will die young, and I'll be left looking after Mum". He argued with me, asking how I could know. I couldn't explain the profound certitude of my feelings.

I don't know what these prescient comments mean other than that sometimes we spontaneously connect to a hidden coincidental continuity that exists parallel to and behind our conscious lives.

My leaving Loup Garou was another example of my letting my brother down. I should have known how important I was to him personally and within that band. I should have been braver and tried to believe what he told me, but my departure from the band meant he shouldered a hefty workload—singing, playing, writing and leading. I think it took a lot out of him. I think it may have hastened his death to some degree. That leaves me with a corrosive, ineffable sadness that I will live with for the rest of my life. Why wasn't I better for him? Why couldn't I imagine myself as he saw me?

This is an early song
I used to play with him
And though he tried so hard
I would not let him
What I'm trying to say
Is I usually wrong
And I'm so very sorry,
Anthony John

About six months before he died, Mick insisted that there should be a video record of "at least some" of the music the two of us had worked on over the years. We were initially reluctant because it had been a few years since we had played together. Finally, we agreed, and without rehearsal, in the living room of the house he was to die in. Subsequently, we recorded life to the camera, doing what we remembered from our repertoire. The songs and their arrangements returned to us as we remembered and played them. There is a communication between siblings that cannot be denied. Voice and spirit combine on a level that is indescribably complete. The video reveals a stiff elder brother and a lithe, liquid younger brother through whom music flows like a river through a valley, and he and I make what, for me, is the best music. I try not to watch it. I try to confine myself to a one-year birthday treat, but I am transported to that moment each time I watch. I am standing beside him, working so hard to provide him with the musical bed he needs to fantasies about. To my surprise, 98 per cent of the time, I do so. Communication between the two of us is as much by facial expression, or the raising of an eyebrow suggesting the next bar we go to the chorus or back to the verse or the solo or the bridge or the end of the song, as verbal. It was as though we had played the songs that morning. It is an honest, no-frills record of two relatively young men loving where and who they were with.

Phil and I were watching some of it a few years ago. I said, " Is it credible to watch. What a guitarist. What a singer. What a writer". Phil said, "Yeah, but look at what you are doing. You are the perfect foil. He couldn't do it without you". That was good enough for me.

I am forever grateful for Mick's insisting that we do it. I have tried to thank him over the years, and I think he understands how important it is to me that there is a visual record of my brother and the two of us playing together. It is close to the most important thing I own. Along with photo albums of my second beautiful family, it is what I would retrieve from a burning house.

****

It is the 16th of August 1988. It is thirty-four years since my brother was born. It is one week before my thirty-seventh birthday. It is the date that Robert Johnson and Elvis Presley died. This year's anniversary sees my brother dead. I have spoken of this event earlier. It is the most scarifying thing I have had to endure. I have never been able to accept that date's absolute, black finality. I think it is an appropriate irony that Tony should die on the same date as these pivotal musical legends. Had circumstances been different, I think his name would have been universally acknowledged in the same way as theirs.

In retrospect, there were signs. Generally speaking, it was usually me that provided "smoke". Over the years, he would have smoked way more of mine than his. This is not a complaint, just an observation. About a week before he died, I was visiting him on my way home. I produced "the good stuff" from my pocket and started "mulling up". He stopped me. Then looked at me and said, "No, I think we'll use mine today. I've smoked more than enough of your dope over the years." I thought it strange and honestly somewhat out of character, but I didn't argue. During the ensuing bong side conversation, we got to talking about near-death experiences. There was a program recently relating to the same on TV. It was pretty much the topic of the moment. At one point, I would like to have an experience". Immediately, he replied, "I'll see what I can do for you". We locked eyes. I had flashes of his trying to tell me something, but I couldn't get the message. He gave me that message a week later.

Over the years, we had been in the habit of giving each other a happy hippy hello hug. On leaving each other's company, we would hug. On this occasion, I was in a hurry to leave. Tony was in another room. I knew exactly where he was and that I could have taken four or five paces, given him a hug and gone on with the rest of my life. Only now, I didn't seek him. I asked myself why not, as I didn't and couldn't come up with an answer. As I left without that parting reaffirmation of soon-to-be renewed friendship, I nearly walked back up the stairs to say goodbye in our now time-honored fashion. I didn't, so I kept walking, got in my car, and drove home.

How deeply I regret not retracing my steps that day. I didn't say goodbye correctly in both the immediate and broader sense. It is as if I am forever reaching out to touch him that final time.

I did touch him one more time, and that was the morning of his death. Linda and I sat in the living room of their small house, with our small world suddenly becoming much smaller; indeed, it seemed to be closing in around me and crushing me. She said, "Let's move Tony out here with us" or words to that effect. Internally, I was reluctant if for no other reason than I had not enjoyed touching him when I had tried, in my own ill-tutored, humble way, to revive him, and in the back of my sadness-soaked brain was the notion that one is "not supposed to move the body".

However, Linda gently insisted. We went into the bathroom where his inert self-lay. Now, it is a blur. I can't remember clearly who took which end of this beautiful human being, but he was soon in the living room, propped up against a sofa at the side of the room. I can't remember if we had shut his eyes. Still, as we continued with our wait for the ambulance, mulling over our mutual grief-empty conversation, he sat, a silent cold presence, just out of earshot yet solar systems away. I found it disconcerting, to say the least. I kept fighting the urge to look at him one more time as though, in the meantime, he had woken up and was ready to sing and play.

The paramedics arrived and asked us all the usual questions. They were worried when it was revealed that he had died in the bathroom, and yet he was sitting up in another room. There was some suspicion of skullduggery, but nothing ever came of it, so they must have accepted that our actions were those of discombobulated grief-stricken brother and lover who were confronting a situation neither had expected nor wanted. Officially, he had died of "undiagnosed hypertension". In other words, his heart, his poor, weak, holed heart, no longer had the heart to keep beating.

Linda and I found Tony slumped in front of the vanity with a large mirror above it. Tony may well have watched himself die. He may have watched himself start again, and as nature knows only transmogrification and no beginning or end, it is arguable that his shining, uplifting essence may well be well and truly embodied again.

Being my brother, Tony was the best and worst thing that has happened to me in my life. The best because he was and the worst for the same reason. When you have been bathed in light, known transcendent happiness, been at one with another, flown where others crawl, it has been tough to walk through the rest of my life. I have a beautiful wife and two talented and beautiful children, but

It's been too many years
Since you left this mortal coil
And I've had all those years of happiness and toil
Without you in my life
Without you in my life
And I know it's very wrong
For me to eulogize
But this is how I feel
And I cannot deny
That you're not in my life
I cannot disguise
That you're not in my life

On the morning of his death, Alana brought our two-year-old daughter, Jessica, in her arms up to where Linda and I were ambulance waiting. Jessica could feel there was something unusual in the behavior of the adults around her. At one point, she saw the propped-up Tony. She could see he was unnaturally still. We tried to explain to her gently and perhaps ourselves what had happened, and all Jessica could say was, "Tony fell".

He had, and my world had. It saddens me that neither of my children will ever know the charming genius who was their Uncle, but perhaps this memoir will give them an inkling of what they missed.

I miss him, and I will until I am missed.

EPILOGUE

It is a few years since I wrote this memoir. He has been dead longer than he was alive. His memory remains as strong as ever. As indicated, I think about him every day. It is probably not healthy. It is probably clinically an obsession but because I write songs like I breath I have written many songs of, for and about him. This song is the most recent of these and I think it effectively speaks to what this memoir is supposed to be. A respectful homage to a magnificent talent.

Nearly the last one left to sing your song
You've been gone far too long
Almost the last one left to sing those songs
Others do them better than me
Try to recall with integrity
As we maintain your legacy
And I cannot say I'm good at that
But it's something I do out of respect
And though I know there's no going back
My heart always denies that fact
Songs too good to disappear
Songs that the world should hear

Then I know that you are near
And I cannot say that I do them well
But it comes from the heart and he could tell
It's been like that since the day you fell
And it is not wrong for me to dwell

www.ingramcontent.com/pod-product-compliance
Lightning Source LLC
Chambersburg PA
CBHW071745120626
46550CB00002B/667